The New Zealand
Vegetable
Book

Published by Hyndman Publishing
325 Purchas Road
RD 2 Amberley 7482

Written by Glenda Gourley

Gardening tips by Dennis Greville

ISBN: 1-877382-59-0

Text & Photography:
© Horticulture New Zealand

This book has been adapted from
'Vegetables – A user's guide' published by
Horticulture New Zealand

Horticulture New Zealand is
an organisation representing
approximately 7000 fruit and
vegetable growers of which
there are approximately 2,800
commercial vegetable growers.
Within this organisation, known
in the industry as HortNZ, the
Fresh Vegetable Product Group
has established a strategy –
vegetables.co.nz – which accepts
a responsibility to promote
fresh vegetables. Vegetables.co.nz
undertakes a range of vegetable
promoting activities and produces
a library of vegetable resources,
including the website
www.vegetables.co.nz.

We are fortunate in New Zealand to have a wide variety of vegetables available to us throughout the year. Whether you enjoy the pleasure of growing your own or simply wish to take advantage of what is seasonally abundant this book will show you how to get the maximum benefit and enjoyment from your vegetables.

Comprehensive detail is provided on each vegetable, including what to look for when purchasing, tips on growing for the gardeners amongst us, how to keep and how to prepare. Additional information on seasonal availability, nutritional value, and ways to eat including photos and delicious recipes makes this an indespensable guide.

Horticulture™
New Zealand

Horticulture New Zealand
P O Box 10232, Wellington, New Zealand
Phone 64 4 472 3795
www.hortnz.co.nz

Contents

Nutrition

In addition to being exceptionally tasty, fresh vegetables make a fantastic food choice by supplying our bodies with a wide range of compounds which help keep us healthy.

In the past much of the goodness of fresh vegetables has been put down to fibre, vitamins and minerals. But it appears now that whilst these nutrients are important, it is phytochemicals that really pack the punch in keeping us healthy. Phytochemicals are natural plant compounds, many of which are responsible for the bright colours in fruits and vegetables. There are literally hundreds of different phytochemicals – all of which are more effective when eaten in the 'raw' state – not supplements. A lot has still to be learnt about the interaction between the phytochemicals. Included in these are antioxidants which are found in abundance in plants. Antioxidants are substances that protect the body by neutralizing free radicals, or unstable oxygen molecules, which can damage cells and lead to poor health.

Eat your colours every day

While we all know that healthy eating is the key to long life, few people understand that natural pigments that make fruit and vegetables so colourful can help protect your body too. With every passing year new evidence adds support to the wisdom of eating a colour packed diet – to protect from cancer, to promote heart health, to reduce hypertension, preserve eyesight and to protect the brain – basically if you eat your colours every day you increase the likelihood that you will stay healthy.

Put simply, the colour concept divides produce into the following groups, and you should aim to select one piece of produce from each group per day. This list is far from comprehensive but gives you the idea…

Red	Orange/ yellow	Brown/ white	Green	Blue/ purple
Radishes	Carrots	Cauliflower	Asparagus	Beetroot
Red kumara	Golden kumara	Mushrooms	Beans	Egg plant
Red peppers	Pumpkin	Onions	Broccoli	Purple cabbage
Red potatoes		Parsnips	Celery	
Tomatoes		White potatoes	Leeks	
			Lettuces	

How many vegetables should you eat?

New Zealand guidelines recommend you need to eat five or more servings of fruit and vegetables every day. Specifically, three or more servings of vegetables and two or more servings of fruit. The recommendation of five servings per day is seen as a minimum requirement for good health.

An easy way to remember this is by looking at your hand. Each finger represents at least one serving of fresh fruit or vegetables. You can easily measure your serving size by imagining what you can fit into the palm of your hand.

Vegetable Nutrients – A Guide

Nutrients	Function	Vegetable
Carotenoids	• Some are converted into vitamin A in the body • Stimulate the growth of new cells and keep them healthy • Important as antioxidant or free radical fighters	• Orange, yellow and green coloured vegetables e.g. pumpkin, carrots, kumara, spinach, parsley, sweetcorn and broccoli • Some red vegetables e.g. red peppers, tomatoes
Vitamin B group	• Releases energy from food • Promotes a healthy nervous system	• Green vegetables
Folic acid	• Important for healthy growth development especially during periods of rapid growth e.g. pregnancy • Promotes a healthy nervous system	• Green vegetables
Vitamin C	• Fights against infection and is used in tissue repair and general health • Helps the body absorb iron from food • Important as antioxidant	• Excellent: red and green capsicum and parsley • Very good: Brussels sprouts, broccoli, cabbage, spinach, cauliflower and radishes • Good: leeks, lettuce, spring onions, kumara, tomatoes, turnips, peas, beans, asparagus and potatoes
Vitamin K	• For clotting of the blood	• Leafy green vegetables, turnips, broccoli, lettuce, cabbage, spinach, asparagus, watercress, peas and beans
Calcium	• Essential for healthy teeth and bones	• Spinach, parsley, broccoli, celery, leeks, spring onions, cabbage, turnips and carrots
Iron	• An important part of red blood cells. Helps carry oxygen around the body. * • Extremely important for brain function and learning	• Spinach, silver beet, parsley, leeks
Potassium	• Controls the working of muscles and nerves • Essential component of every cell	• All vegetables
Fibre	• Maintains a healthy digestive system • Is important in control of weight	• All vegetables

* Absorption of iron is increased when vegetables containing iron are consumed at the same time as vitamin C rich foods.

Antioxidants

Antioxidants abound in vegetables. Studies have observed an association between lower rates of some of the major chronic diseases with higher consumption of vegetables and scientists have subsequently sought to explain why this might be. It is thought that antioxidants have many roles in the body – some antioxidants prevent damage, some stop damage while it is taking place and some facilitate repair.

For example, antioxidants may protect against cardiovascular disease by preventing the oxidation of fats, which is part of the process of atherosclerosis (the build-up of fat cells in blood vessels, commonly known as 'hardening of the arteries'). Free radical attack may also result in DNA damage, one of many factors that can lead to cancer.

carotenoids
Beta-carotene: In green vegetables, yellow or orange fruit and vegetables
Lycopene: In tomatoes, watermelon, many pink fruits
Lutein: In leafy vegetables (the darker green the better)

vitamins
Vitamin C: In fruit and vegetables, especially citrus and berryfruits: also potatoes
Vitamin E: In grains, nuts, wheatgerm and vegetable oils

other
Lignans: In linseed, sesame seed, bran, whole grains, beans, vegetables
Lipoic acid: In green vegetables, tomatoes, rice bran
Coenzyme Q (ubiquinone): In meat, fish, vegetable oils, wheatgerm, rice bran

dietary antioxidants
at a glance

flavonoids and other phenolics
Anthocyanins: In red wine, red grapes, berryfruit
Phenolic acids: In most fruit and vegetables
Isoflavones: In pulses, especially soybeans
Flavonols: In onions and asparagus
Catechins: In tea and chocolate
Flavones: In citrus fruits

sulphur compounds
Allium sulphur compounds: In garlic, onions, and leeks
Glucosinolates/isothyocyanates: In brassicas, e.g. broccoli, cabbage, cauliflower

trace elements
Selenium: In seafood
Zinc: In seafood, lean meat, milk, grains, lentils and nuts

Source: Crop and Food Research NZ

Seasonal availability

This chart is a guide only. Variations will occur in different growing regions and with weather conditions in a particular season.

	JAN	FEB	MAR	APR	MAY	JUN	JUL	AUG	SEP	OCT	NOV	DEC
ARTICHOKES - Globe												
ARTICHOKES - Jerusalem												
ASIAN GREENS												
ASPARAGUS												
BEANS												
BEETROOT												
BROCCOLI												
BROCCOLINI												
BRUSSELS SPROUTS												
BUTTERCUP SQUASH												
BUTTERNUT												
CABBAGES												
CAPSICUMS												
CARROTS												
CAULIFLOWER												
CELERY												
CHILLIES												
CHOKOS												
COURGETTES												
CUCUMBERS - short												
CUCUMBERS - telegraph												
EGG PLANT												
FENNEL												
GARLIC												
GINGER												
HERBS												
KOHLRABI												
KUMARA												
LEEKS												
LETTUCE												
MELONS												
MUSHROOMS												
OKRA												
ONIONS												
PARSNIPS												
PEAS												
POTATOES												
POTATOES - new season												
PUHA												
PUMPKIN												
RADISHES												
ROCKET												
RHUBARB												
SALAD GREENS												
SILVER BEET												
SNOW PEAS												
SPINACH												
SPRING ONIONS												
SPROUTED BEANS AND SEEDS												
SWEDES												
SWEETCORN												
TARO												
TOMATOES												
TURNIPS												
WATERCRESS												
WITLOOF												
YAMS												

Legend:
- UNAVAILABLE
- SHORT SUPPLY
- PLENTIFUL

Maintaining quality

Even after harvest vegetables are alive. The best that can be done is to slow down the rate of deterioration – it can't be stopped completely. Deterioration of vegetables is caused by both chemical and biological reactions.

Biological

Vegetables are subject to biological deterioration because they are composed of living tissues and they continue to respire after harvesting. Vegetables are alive and breathing, with a continued need for oxygen. In respiration, stored food such as sugar is used for energy and the product loses food value quickly. Vegetables that respire fast perish soon after picking. Respiration is slowed by refrigeration.

Vegetables are also covered with micro-organisms, which will cause decay in the right conditions of warmth and humidity. Damage, which breaks the skin and allows the entrance of organisms, will result in decay. Refrigeration is the best method of reducing decay, as most micro-organisms will slow down their growth at low temperatures.

Chemical

Ethylene is a natural product gas, given off by vegetables which hastens both ripening and deterioration. Different vegetables respond differently to ethylene. Some vegetables produce ethylene and some are sensitive to ethylene. Ethylene-producing and ethylene-sensitive vegetables need to be stored separately.

Ethylene-producing: apples, tomatoes, passionfruit, stone fruit, bananas, avocados, pawpaw, kiwifruit, pears, melons. Ethylene-sensitive: Asian greens, globe artichoke, asparagus, beans, broccoli, Brussels sprouts, corn, cabbage, carrot, cauliflower, celery, courgette, cucumber, egg plant, kumara, lettuce, parsley, peas, potato, rhubarb, silver beet, spinach.

Refrigeration also slows deterioration caused by chemical and biological reactions. For example, sweetcorn may lose 50% of its initial sugar content in a single day at 21°C, while only 5% will be lost in one day at 0°C. With certain exceptions the best temperature for retarding deterioration by biological reactions is 1°C above freezing point.

Many colour changes associated with aging and ripening can also be delayed and slowed by refrigeration.

Loss of moisture, with consequent wilting and shrivelling, is one of the obvious ways in which freshness is lost. This water loss in the vapour state from living tissues is known as transpiration. Moisture losses from 3–6% are enough to cause a marked loss in quality for many vegetables.

The effect of rough handling is cumulative. Bruising stimulates the rate of respiration and hence shortens the potential shelf life. Damage also results in more moisture loss and flavour changes.

Buying vegetables

- Choose a reputable supplier who you can rely on.
- Buy regularly, every 2–3 days if possible. It is better to buy smaller quantities more often as there is no doubt, fresher does taste better!
- Reject and/or return inferior quality.

"No matter how clever you are as a chef or cook, you can't produce quality if you don't start with it."

Storing vegetables

- Handle with care. Bad handling accelerates deterioration; all vegetables should be handled as if they are as fragile as eggs.
- Store vegetables correctly. Storage conditions greatly affect shelf life. As soon as possible after purchase and transit the produce should be transferred to the correct storage conditions e.g. greens refrigerated, potatoes to a cool dark place. Each hour with produce sitting at inappropriate temperatures decreases shelf life dramatically. Refer to each vegetable for specific details.
- Use the chiller properly. Air must be able to circulate around the vegetables, hot spots will develop if over-packed.
- Keep all storage areas clean. Decaying or rotting produce releases ethylene.
- Store ethylene-producing and ethylene-sensitive produce separately if practical. While separate storage is preferable, some smaller operations may not have the facilities to do this. Ensure that the store room is ventilated regularly to avoid ethylene build up. Low temperatures retard ethylene damage.

Cooking guide

For all cooking methods:

- Select the best quality
- Store correctly until use
- Wash thoroughly
- Cut into evenly sized pieces
- Leave skin on if suitable
- Prepare as close to cooking time as possible
- Cook until tender but still slightly crisp

Baking

- Preheat the oven to 200°C.
- Some vegetables need special attention e.g. seeds are removed from pumpkin.
- Bake until softened when tested with a fork.
- As a guide, a medium sized potato will take 45–55 minutes.
- Vegetables can be baked in a glaze, marinade or sauce.
- Remove seeds and stuff vegetables prior to baking e.g. marrow, pepper, tomatoes and pumpkins.

Boiling

- As a general rule, if the vegetable grows above the ground place into boiling water, if it grows below the ground, begin cooking in cold water. The exception is corn on the cob which is placed in cold water.
- Add 2–3cm of water in a saucepan, add vegetables.
- Cover tightly and bring to the boil as quickly as possible, reduce heat and simmer gently. Cook green vegetables without a lid for vibrant colour.
- Cook until tender when tested with a fork. Vigorous boiling will cause some vegetables, especially potatoes, to break up. Add extra boiling water if necessary. Drain and serve.

Braising

- Choose a braising pan with a close fitting lid.
- Add vegetables to the pan and a flavoursome liquid or stock to come half way up the vegetables, cover tightly.
- For best results braise slowly, add extra liquid if required.

Deep frying

- Always use fresh clean oil, check the smoke point of the oil to ensure it is suitable for deep frying.
- Heat the oil to correct temperature before adding vegetables (chips should be cooked at 175–180°C for 3–4 minutes – see www.chipgroup.co.nz for more tips on how to deep fry chips).
- Coat or batter vegetables, except chips, before adding to the oil.
- Batch cook vegetables and ensure the oil returns to temperature before adding the next batch.
- Drain on absorbent paper.

Grilling, char grilling or barbecuing

- Preheat the grill or plate.
- Cook under, or over, direct heat, turn during cooking.
- Cooking times vary depending on the intensity of the heat and the size of the pieces of vegetables.
- Pre or partly cook dense vegetables, e.g. kumara, carrot or potato, if you want to save cooking time, alternatively just slice thinly.
- During cooking the vegetables may be basted with oil, flavoured oil or marinade.

Microwaving

- Cut all pieces to a uniform size to ensure even cooking – very important.
- Use only a small quantity of water. Usually the water left clinging to the leaves after washing is sufficient.
- Pierce whole or unpeeled vegetables before cooking to prevent bursting.
- Cook vegetables on high power (100%) or automatic function, if possible, to take out guesswork.
- Cover the dish with a plate, lid or plastic film to speed cooking and to keep the vegetables moist.
- Arrange vegetables with the thickest stalks or spears, which need the most cooking, towards the outside of the dish.
- Microwaved vegetables continue cooking for an extra 2–4 minutes after the cooking period is finished. Allow for this to avoid overcooking.
- Season vegetables after cooking. Salting may cause vegetables to lose moisture during cooking.

Microwave ovens cook food by using microwaves which penetrate the food and cause the moisture molecules to vibrate and heat up. The more water in the food the more quickly it cooks. Most vegetables are more than 90% water so they cook quickly. The power supply to microwave ovens varies; consult your manual for specific cooking times. Cooking times also depend on:

- size of vegetables
- quantity being cooked
- their density and moisture content
- the characteristics of your oven
- any power fluctuations in your area.

Roasting

- Preheat the oven to 200°C.
- Using different cuts, such as thin slices of kumara or pumpkin, not only shortens cooking time but adds variety and interest.
- Wash and dry vegetables.
- Use only a small amount of vegetable oil.
- Place in a roasting dish or on a tray.
- Bake until tender.
- Cook the vegetables in a separate pan from meat and they won't soak up the fat.

Slow roasting, at around 150°C, is a popular cooking method that intensifies flavours. It is particularly good with tomatoes and some of the less traditionally roasted vegetables such as asparagus and peppers. Drizzle with olive oil, perhaps with a dash of balsamic vinegar, and sprinkle with black pepper. Roast until the product is shrivelled, but not dried out. Slow roasted vegetables are great as is, or tossed through leafy greens.

Salads

- Use a sharp knife.
- When using salad greens, make sure they are well dried after washing. Water left on the leaves after washing will result in diluted dressings, hence diluted flavour.
- Dress salads with dense vegetables ahead of time to allow the flavours to be absorbed.
- Leafy salads need to be dressed just before service.

Sautéing

- Small pieces of vegetables are pan fried in hot oil. They are tossed during cooking.

Shallow frying

- Season foods before frying.
- Use the correct size pan for the food being cooked e.g. don't overcrowd, fry in batches.
- Heat oil to the correct temperature before adding vegetables.
- Drain on absorbent paper if necessary.

Steaming

- Place in a steamer over rapidly boiling water. Avoid the water touching the vegetables. Cover and adjust the heat to a steady simmer. Cook until tender. Add more boiling water if necessary.
- If using a combi oven, follow the manufacturer's instructions.

Stir-frying

- Prepare all vegetables before starting to cook.
- Shred, dice or thinly slice the vegetables into pieces the same size.
- Have the oil in the pan very hot before adding the vegetables.
- When the oil dries out add a sprinkling of water. Best results are achieved if the vegetables are 'hot and steamy'.
- Cook the dense vegetables (those that take longer to cook e.g. carrot) and add the less dense ones towards the end of cooking (e.g. cabbage).
- Stir-frying vegetables is quick. Prepare the rest of the meal first and serve immediately after cooking.

Stir-fried vegetables are cooked rapidly in a minimum of liquid, or oil, so fewer nutrients are lost or destroyed.

Which cooking methods to use

Most vegetables suit many different cooking methods; in fact the versatility of preparation, cooking and serving is a fantastic attribute of vegetables. Think variety, think vegetables.

Cooking times

Dense vegetables require longer cooking times e.g. carrots, potatoes, kumara. Vegetables with higher water content cook faster e.g. capsicum, leafy greens.

Classification of vegetables

Vegetables are classified according to which part of the plant is eaten. Some vegetables may fall into more than one classification when more than one part of the plant is eaten e.g. roots and leaves of beetroot can be eaten.

VEGETABLE GROUPS

- Roots: e.g. carrot, parsnip
- Seeds and pods: e.g. peas, beans
- Leaves: e.g. spinach, lettuce, Brussels sprouts
- Fruits: e.g. egg plant, tomatoes
- Bulbs: e.g. garlic, onion, leek
- Tubers: e.g. potatoes, kumara, yams
- Flowers: e.g. cauliflower, broccoli
- Stems: e.g. celery, asparagus
- Fungi: e.g. mushrooms

Vegetable cuts

The vegetable cut selected for a particular dish must complement the dish it is being used for. For example, a robust casserole would require larger pieces than a light consommé. Many other loose descriptions exist e.g. strips, bite-sized pieces, chunks.

Here are the traditional cuts and whilst these definitions may vary slightly, these are the accepted generalisations.

Matignon

Roughly cut vegetables, normally including carrot, onion and celery, which are cooked in butter with ham, thyme and bay leaf. Cooking is finished by deglazing the pan with Madeira. Matignon vegetables are used to add flavour when cooking large pieces of meat. Thin even slices of vegetables are used as a base to place the meat on when roasting.

Jardinière

A long thin baton, about 2cm long and approximately 3mm wide and 3mm thick. In more recent times these are often slightly larger, but this depends on end use.

Brunoise

This is a very small diced cube, sized between 1–3mm square. It is often used as a garnish for consommé. Typical vegetables used are carrot, onion, turnip and celery.

Julienne

Long thin match-stick shaped pieces about 4cm in length.

Mirepoix

A mixture of roughly chopped vegetables which are used as the base of sauces or to enhance the flavour of meat, fish and shellfish dishes. Normally onion, celery and carrot are used and these are slowly cooked in butter until they are very tender. Thyme and bay leaves are often added.

Chiffonade

Finely sliced or shredded green leafy vegetables, usually lettuce or spinach, which is used as a base, garnish or in soups.

Macedoine

This is diced cube, 0.5cm (5mm) square, which is larger than the brunoise cut. Typical vegetables used are carrot, onion, turnip, beans and celery.

Paysanne

This cut may be either squares, triangles, circles or half rounds. In order to cut economically, the shape of the vegetable will decide which shape to choose. All are cut thinly, about 1–2mm thick.

Artichokes

There are two well-known varieties, Globe and Jerusalem artichokes which are really quite different vegetables in terms of appearance, texture and preparation, although there are subtle taste similarities – hence the similar naming.

Globe artichokes

Globe artichokes have always been considered a delicacy. They have been grown in Southern Europe for many centuries. The part that is eaten is the immature flower bud before the flower appears while it consists of overlapping green/purple scales. In New Zealand you will sometimes see them marketed as green globe artichokes. Baby artichokes, sized between golf balls and eggs, are sometimes available.

Artichokes contain an unusual organic acid called cynarin which has an effect on tasting and is thought to be the reason why many people think that water tastes sweet when drunk after eating artichokes. The flavour of wine is similarly altered and many wine experts think that wine shouldn't accompany artichokes. Some think cynarin may have health benefits in use against diseases of liver and gall bladder.

Globe artichokes

WHAT TO LOOK FOR
Globe artichokes should have a good fresh bright colour, tightly closed leaves, and feel solid, not loose.

HOW TO KEEP
Put in the fridge in a vented plastic bag or the crisper. They damage easily so handle them with care. Best eaten within 2–3 days.

NUTRITIONAL VALUE
Globe artichokes are a good source of folate, and some other B group vitamins and fibre.

HOW TO PREPARE
Remove the stalk, trim the base, tough outer leaves and tips of the remaining leaves. Remove the inedible choke, except on small, young artichokes. The choke is the furry flower part sitting on top of the heart. The heart is the firm base plate and is the best eating. This choke may be removed before or after cooking, depending on how you are using the artichoke.

WAYS TO EAT THIS VEGETABLE
Steam, boil or microwave, adding lemon juice to the cooking water to prevent browning. Test to check if cooked by pulling one of the outer leaves. If it comes away readily it is cooked, alternatively until the stem end is tender when pierced with a skewer. Steaming and boiling will take about 20 minutes. Microwaving will take about 7–8 minutes per artichoke. Serve cooked artichokes with melted butter, hollandaise or a vinaigrette sauce. They can also be stuffed, fried, baked, used in salads and eaten hot or cold. They are most commonly eaten as an entree or side dish. When eating an artichoke, pull off the leaves one by one and scrape them between the teeth to remove the fleshy base. Discard the rest of the leaf.

AVAILABLE TO PURCHASE
Globe artichokes: mainly from October until December, with a limited supply in September and January and February.

TIPS
FOR HOME
GARDENERS

Suitable to plant: artichokes are easy to grow throughout the country.

When to plant: artichokes bear best the second year and should be refreshed from seed or suckers in spring every three to four years.

Approx time till harvest: timing from planting to harvest is 50 to 100 days. The first edible heads will usually take at least a year to form when they are grown from seed.

Depth to plant: plants do best when they are planted shallowly in well-drained soil.

Spacing between rows: a free flow of air is important around plants.

Spacing between plants: depending on the variety one plant can grow over 2 metres high and almost as wide. Artichokes are perennial plants.

Water requirements: plants that are watered sparingly in spring then regularly in summer produce succulent flower heads.

Grandma's vegetable soup

This recipe is an oldie but a goodie! Most soup recipes make enough to serve 6 or more; don't worry if you have some left over. Soups often taste even better the next day, and they all freeze well.

2 Tbsp oil

1 onion, peeled and chopped

2 each of carrots, kumara and potato, washed and chopped

3 stalks celery, including leaves, chopped

1–2 cups peeled and chopped pumpkin

4 artichokes, scrubbed and chopped

6 cups vegetable stock, OR 1 packet spring vegetable soup and 6 cups water

Heat the oil in a saucepan and sauté the onion and carrot for 3–4 minutes. Add the remaining vegetables and sauté for 4–5 minutes. Add the stock and simmer gently for 15 minutes or until the vegetables are tender. Purée if you prefer a smooth soup. Season to taste. Serves 6.

WHAT TO LOOK FOR
All Asian greens should be clean, fresh and crisp. If they are flowering it is preferable that the flowers are in bud rather than full bloom.

HOW TO KEEP
Refrigerate in plastic bags.

NUTRITIONAL VALUE
Asian greens are highly nutritious. Most Asian greens are an excellent source of vitamin C and most are good sources of vitamin A and many antioxidants. The darker the colour, the higher the antioxidant levels. With the exception of Chinese cabbage, Asian greens are a good source of iron. Chrysanthemum leaves, mustard cabbage, tat soi and Chinese broccoli also provide calcium. All Asian greens supply folate and are a good fibre source.

HOW TO PREPARE
See individual types opposite.

AVAILABLE TO PURCHASE
A selection of Asian greens will be available all year round.

Asian vegetables

Asian vegetables have been in New Zealand since the Chinese first settled here in the late 1800s, but it is only in relatively recent years that they have become commercially available. There is an overwhelming array of literally hundreds of varieties of Asian vegetables and you may find ones other than those listed here, however these do represent the most commonly found varieties. Choy is the Chinese word for any leafy vegetable. Most Asian greens have also been called cabbage – even though none of them actually resemble Western cabbage as we know it. The naming of Asian vegetables can sometimes be confusing as they often have different names in different parts of China. For example, Chinese white cabbage might be called bok choy, buk choy, pak choy or baak choi. When using them for the first time it is good to know that Asian greens respond well to being cooked in a moist heat - just remember they like to be hot and steamy! Obviously these vegetables team well with all the usual Asian condiments – soy, ginger, black bean, Hoisin, oyster, garlic, chillies etc.

Chinese white cabbage

(bok choy, buk choy, pak choy, baak choi)

There are many varieties, though the most common in New Zealand is the white bok choy which has a thick white stem and smooth round leaves. The stems are crisp and juicy and the leaves are a bit like cabbage or silver beet. Sometimes Shanghai bok choy can be found, which has thick green stems and similar leaves but is generally smaller in size. All types of bok choy are suitable for quick cooking methods such as steaming and stir-frying. Use in the same way as you would cabbage or spinach. Miniature bok choy leaves are used in some green salad mixes.

Water spinach

(ong choi)

The stems are hollow and the leaves are arrow shaped. The taste is vaguely similar to spinach. The shorter the stalks and the larger the leaves at the tip, the more tender the leaves. Discard the lowest 5–6cm of stem if they are too tough or fibrous. Chop stems into thirds, keeping the stem and leaves roughly separated and begin by cooking the stems so they can cook longer before adding the leaves. Water spinach is used in a variety of ways – in soups, stir-fried, raw etc. Try it stir-fried with garlic and chilli, and stir in coconut cream once the leaves are wilted.

Garland chrysanthemum

(tung ho, tong ho, chong ho or thong ho)

The leafy stalks of chrysanthemum look a bit like Chinese cabbage, but the leaves are bluntly lobed and the stalks are more like a lettuce and feel slightly rough in texture. Chrysanthemum leaves have a subtle but distinct `floral' flavour which is best enjoyed in small quantities, accompanied by other flavours and cooked only briefly. Chrysanthemum is a winter vegetable which is generally used in a stir-fry or in a soup.

Chinese box thorn

(gau gei choi)

This vegetable has a straight unbranched stem and is closely covered by small oval leaves and, in some varieties, thorns. The branches are usually about 25–30cm long. Use only the leaves, discard the stems. This is generally used only for soups where it imparts a distinct flavour. Supply is limited.

Peking cabbage

(wong nga pak, wong nga baak or wong bok)

This Chinese cabbage is one of the most common Asian vegetables found in New Zealand. There are many different varieties grown but probably only two or three reach retail stores on a regular basis. Peking cabbage has an elongated head with pale green leaves which form a compact head. Select heavy, compact heads with crisp whole leaves. The stalks should be crisp and juicy and the leaves not unlike cos lettuce. Wong nga pak can be used raw in salads or cooked in all sorts of ways, but it is used most commonly in fast cooking methods such as stir-frying.

Chinese broccoli

(Chinese sprouting broccoli, Chinese kale (gaai laan))

Chinese broccoli has long green stems (about 2cm in diameter and 20cm long), white flowers, and green leaves which have a white haze on them. The flowers should be in bud rather than in full bloom. To prepare, chop the leaves roughly. Peel the stem to get rid of the fibrous layer and cut it into evenly-sized pieces. Stir-frying or steaming are the most commonly used preparation methods. It has a very strong broccoli flavour and can be used where you would normally use broccoli.

Mustard cabbage
(gai choi, or kai choy)

There are many varieties of mustard cabbage – some are grown for their oil, others for seed and others for their highly nutritious mustard flavoured leaves. Most mustard cabbages are only found in Asian markets and the leaves are used mainly in stir-fries, pickles or soups. Traditionally it is poached in chicken stock and served as a broth. The most commonly found mustard is the large-leafed Swatow variety with thick fleshy ribs, which is usually the same 'grass green' from base to tip.

Amaranth
(Chinese spinach and en choy)

There are many varieties of amaranth grown and they are sold in bunches with the roots still attached. The green leaves with the deep red coloured veins distinguish red amaranth from other Asian greens. You can get green amaranth as well. Cook the same way as you would spinach. It suits short quick moist cooking methods although it does go well in soups. Nutritionally it is amazingly rich in nutrients.

Fuzzy melon
(hairy melon)

This hairy green-skinned gourd is shaped like a marrow or overgrown egg plant. The skin is edible but it tends to be peeled or needs to have the hairs rubbed off with a paper towel. The flesh has a fresh cucumber type taste with a marrow-like texture. Remove the seeds and treat as you would a marrow. They are able to be stuffed or cut into slices and stir-fried or added to soups.

Flowering Chinese cabbage
(choy sum or choi sum)

Flowering Chinese cabbage has pale yellow flowers on long thin green stems (about 75mm diameter and 15–20cm long) with small green leaves. It is available all year round. Prepare flowering Chinese cabbage as you would broccoli and, like broccoli, it is suitable for quick cooking methods. You use all parts of the stem, including the flowers. It's best to eat choy sum when the flowers are in bud rather than in full bloom.

Chinese flat cabbage
(Tat soi (Japanese name), Rosette bok choy or taai goo choi)

This flat cabbage grows round and relatively flat like a plate. The texture is slightly tougher than Chinese white cabbage and the flavour is stronger. Select smaller plants with many young leaves clustered at the centre. Like the other cabbages, Chinese flat cabbage suits quick moist cooking methods, although the young centre leaves can be used raw in a salad. Miniature tat soi is regularly found in mesclun salad mixes.

TIPS FOR HOME GARDENERS

Oriental vegetables are no different from any other vegetables in their basic requirements. Many are easy to grow and quick to crop and resent 'stop-go' watering. Most of these vegetables are annuals that require a rich soil, good drainage and a sunny part of the garden in order to thrive. It is important to ensure that these plants grow quickly so that they remain sweet without a hint of bitterness and also remain crisp and firm.

Some, such as water spinach (kang kong), are perennial and require special conditions if they are to thrive. Many are best planted in spring or autumn and many of the cabbage family such as pak choy, bok choi, Chinese mustard, the edible chrysanthemum and the long white daikon radish will grow through the winter providing valuable additions to your diet.

Greens in five spice

Chinese five spice is great on stir-fried vegetables – a sprinkle gives you a stunning taste. For best flavour make sure the greens are not overcooked and that you serve them as soon as they are cooked.

2 onions, peeled and cut into wedges

3–4 cloves garlic, finely chopped

2 Tbsp oil

6 cups assorted Asian greens e.g. Chinese white cabbage (baak choi, bak choy, pak choy), flowering Chinese cabbage (choi sum) or Peking cabbage (wong nga baak)

¼ tsp Chinese five spice

Stir-fry the onions and garlic in the oil for 4–5 minutes. If the leaves of the Asian greens are small, leave them whole and cut off the thick base of the stalks. Add the Asian greens and five spice. Stir-fry for 2–3 minutes, stirring continuously.

Asparagus

Asparagus originated in the Eastern Mediterranean and was a favourite of the Greeks and Romans who used it as a medicine. In parts of Europe, Turkey, Africa, the Middle East and Asia some varieties of asparagus grow wild.

In some countries people prefer to eat white asparagus (it stays white because it is grown out of the sun), but in New Zealand we like it green and there is little, if any, white grown. Purple asparagus is becoming increasingly available in New Zealand.

WHAT TO LOOK FOR

Choose straight firm green stems. Insist on fresh, clean product with trimmed ends and a minimum of white butt. Fresh asparagus is 'squeaky' – when the spears are gently rubbed they squeak! Old asparagus is rubbery and doesn't squeak.

Buy small quantities regularly. Whilst asparagus will keep for about a week, it is tastes a lot better when eaten in one to two days.

HOW TO KEEP

Asparagus has a high water content and will lose water if stored in a dry environment. Keep refrigerated with butt ends either wrapped in wet paper towels, or stood up in a jar of 1–2cm of water – just like flowers in a vase. Another method, but not quite as effective, is to simply refrigerate in plastic bags.

NUTRITIONAL VALUE

Asparagus is an excellent source of antioxidants, particularly the phenolic group, carotenoids and vitamin C. One of the best natural sources of folate, asparagus is also a source of vitamin K and fibre.

HOW TO PREPARE

Snap off tough ends. These ends could be used to flavour soups or stocks. Cooked asparagus should be tender but still slightly crisp. For maximum flavour, don't overcook it. Asparagus in salads is generally blanched, however if the asparagus is thin and fresh it may

be used raw. Purple asparagus is often eaten raw as it is sweeter and more tender than green. To retain the purple colour when cooked you need to add a little lemon juice or vinegar and cook for a very short time using a method such as stir-frying.

WAYS TO EAT THIS VEGETABLE
Lightly steam, stir-fry, microwave or boil asparagus. Bake or barbecue in a glaze. You can serve it by itself or with a simple sauce. Asparagus can be used in all sorts of dishes – soups, quiches, pies, salads, stir-fries, casseroles and with fresh bread.

AVAILABLE TO PURCHASE
The first of the season is usually available in August, with main supplies starting in September. Supply dwindles again in December, with some usually being still available in January.

TIPS
FOR HOME
GARDENERS

Suitable to plant: perennial and easy to grow from seed or roots.

When to plant: plant in winter.

Approx time till harvest: several years before harvest is recommended.

Depth to plant: 20cm depending on plant size.

Spacing between rows: 500cm.

Spacing between plants: 300cm.

Water requirements: asparagus responds to regular watering, manuring and feeding with liquid fertiliser.

Asparagus and potato salad

The secret of this salad is using lovely new season waxy potatoes! You can use the asparagus raw, especially the purple variety.

2 x 250g bunches asparagus
400g waxy potatoes, scrubbed and cooked
4 or 5 small tomatoes, cut into chunky slices
½ cup bought herb vinaigrette OR make your own:
¼ cup lemon juice or cider vinegar
¼ cup olive oil
2 Tbsp sugar
1–2 cloves garlic, finely chopped
2 Tbsp finely chopped fresh parsley

Cut the asparagus stems in thirds. Cook in boiling water for 3–4 minutes. Cool under cold running water. If making your own vinaigrette, mix the lemon juice, oil, sugar, garlic and parsley together. Cut the warm potatoes into halves or quarters. Place the potatoes, asparagus and tomatoes on a serving platter. Pour over the vinaigrette and set aside to cool. Turn gently once or twice. Serves 4.

Beans

There are many varieties of beans. Most of them can be traced back to their origins in Central and South America.

Green beans
(runner or dwarf beans)

They are usually about 10–15cm in length and 1cm in diameter and the pods are rounded. It is not necessary to remove any strings as these pods are quite tender. The complete pod is eaten although you may wish to trim the ends.

French or flat beans

Usually about 15cm in length, they are a flat pod with slightly ridged sides. Most newer cultivars have few or no strings so the complete pod is eaten although you may wish to trim the ends.

Snake or Chinese beans

These are sometimes known as yard-long beans, asparagus beans or long podded cow peas. These green beans are similar to regular green beans but are very long (about 30–50cm). Supply is limited. They are used traditionally in Asian and Indian cooking.

Butter beans

Similar in shape to the regular green beans but are very pale yellow/cream colour. The complete pod is eaten although you may wish to trim the ends.

Broad beans

If the beans are immature the pod may be eaten. When fully grown only the large and flat beans are eaten and the pod is discarded. The inside of the pod is soft and furry. To shell the beans quickly run a vegetable peeler down the seam.

WHAT TO LOOK FOR
Beans are best when they are young. Look for fresh and tender pods which make a good 'snapping' sound when broken. Broad beans should be slightly plump with a gloss still on the skin, of a good green colour and not too big.

HOW TO KEEP
Refrigerate in plastic bags. Use promptly.

HOW TO PREPARE
Top and tail (cut the ends off) then slice or leave whole. Broad beans need podding, except when they are very young.

Green beans

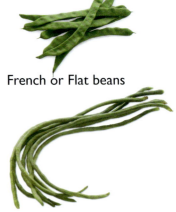

French or Flat beans

Snake or Chinese beans

Butter beans

Broad beans

WAYS TO EAT THIS VEGETABLE

Beans can be boiled, stir-fried, steamed or microwaved. Their taste is at its best when they are cooked so that they are tender and still very slightly crisp. They are great as a side vegetable and are particularly nice when sprinkled with chopped nuts or fresh herbs. Cold, raw or blanched, they are good in a salad or used as a crudité with a dipping sauce. Broad beans are generally served as a side vegetable with a sauce – cheese, curry, mustard or herb-flavoured, or perhaps tossed in citrus juice and sprinkled with rind.

NUTRITIONAL VALUE

The major nutrients in beans are folate, vitamins A (through β-carotene) and C, with thiamine, niacin, calcium, zinc and iron present at low levels. They are a good source of fibre and are low in calories.

The main phytochemicals are the carotenoids (α-carotene, β-carotene, lutein and zeaxanthin) with reasonably high levels of flavonoids.

AVAILABLE TO PURCHASE

Beans are available from November until May, however they are more plentiful in the summer months. Broad beans are available early in the season.

TIPS
FOR HOME
GARDENERS

Suitable to plant: nationwide when the soil has warmed.

When to plant: spring and summer.

Approx time till harvest: 8–10 weeks.

Depth to plant: 5cm.

Spacing between rows: 20cm.

Spacing between plants: 8cm.

Water requirements: all beans enjoy regular watering especially when the weather is hot and dry.

Bean tin foil parcels

Tin foil parcels are easy, succulent and full of flavour.

30–40 beans, trimmed

Cut the beans into pieces the same size. Place the prepared beans on a large piece of tinfoil. Add a sprinkling of oil or 1 or 2 dabs of butter. Season generously with freshly ground black pepper and sesame seeds. Fold up to form a secure watertight parcel. Barbecue for about the same time as you would stir-fry the beans, turning over several times during cooking.

Beetroot

WHAT TO LOOK FOR

Roots should be smooth with a firm skin and deep red colour. The leaves, if they're still attached, should not be floppy. They should be bright green with pink/red veins. Avoid roots with scaly areas around the top surface as they tend to be tougher. Do not trim the flesh of the root or it will cause the beetroot to 'bleed'. Buy small quantities regularly to guarantee freshness.

HOW TO KEEP

The roots should be put in the fridge in the crisper. Don't wrap them. The leaves should be put in the fridge too, but in a plastic bag.

NUTRITIONAL VALUE

Beetroot contains some fibre, potassium and B group vitamins – particularly folate. It also contributes a small amount of iron and vitamin C. Beetroot contains a unique group of red pigments called the betalains, which are responsible for the vegetable's high antioxidant potency.

HOW TO PREPARE

When you are boiling beetroot, try not to break the skin or it will bleed and lose its colour. Before baking or microwaving, however, you must pierce the skin or the beetroot may explode. The skin is easily removed once it's cooked; cool and rub it off with your fingers. Wear rubber gloves to prevent staining your hands.

A native of Southern Europe, beetroot has a vibrant crimson colour coming from pigments not seen in any other vegetable. Originally the leaves were preferred for eating more than the roots, but in New Zealand it is normally just the roots which are eaten – although in some countries all parts of the beetroot are regularly eaten. It is one of the few vegetables that is consumed more frequently pickled than in other ways.

Several varieties are commonly available with roots varying in shape from round to spherical. Flavour variations are very subtle.
A golden beet variety exists but this is seldom seen in New Zealand.

WAYS TO EAT THIS VEGETABLE

Beetroot can be boiled, steamed or microwaved. Baked beetroot served with sour cream with a hint of horseradish or lemon rind is delicious. The roots can be used raw, grated or finely sliced into a salad. The leaves can be prepared like spinach, either boiled, steamed, microwaved or stir-fried.

AVAILABLE TO PURCHASE

You can buy beetroot all year round. It's most plentiful from November until April.

TIPS
FOR HOME
GARDENERS

Suitable to plant: nationwide.

When to plant: sow or plant in spring, summer or autumn. Winter sowings are possible in warm areas.

Approx time till harvest: 6–8 weeks.

Depth to plant: 5cm.

Spacing between rows: 30cm.

Spacing between plants: 20cm.

Water requirements: soak seed overnight before sowing. Provide growing plants with regular quantities of water. Fortnightly applications of liquid fertiliser will also boost growth.

Beetroot with horseradish cream

Sweet and mild – despite its dramatic appearance!

4 medium beetroot (600g)

½ cup light sour cream

1–2 Tbsp prepared horseradish cream

1 Tbsp chopped chives

Scrub the beetroot, peel only if the skin is very tough. Trim the stalk and root. Arrange the beetroot in a microwave-proof dish. Add ½ cup water, cover and microwave on high power for 10–12 minutes or until the beetroot is tender. Stand 4 minutes. Mix the sour cream and horseradish cream together. Place the beetroot onto a serving plate and make a deep cross-shaped cut into each beetroot and pour the horseradish mixture over. Sprinkle with chives. Serves 4.

Broccoli

Broccoli means 'little sprouts' in Italian. It's part of the Brassica family of vegetables which includes cauliflower, cabbage, Brussels sprouts, broccoflower, Asian varieties of cabbage and broccoli, turnips and swedes.

Popular and widely eaten with a distinctive 'mustardy' taste, broccoli has strong health benefits. The stalks, buds and most of the leaves of broccoli are edible.

Sprouting broccoli
(or calabrese)

This is the most popular variety which we commonly refer to simply as broccoli. It has dark bluish-green heads with firm stalks which snap easily. Avoid broccoli showing yellowed leaves or yellow flowers through the buds.

Romanesco broccoli

Romanesco broccoli is a variety which has light green clusters of heads that are pointed and look a bit like coral. Supply is limited.

Broccolini

A natural cross between broccoli and Chinese broccoli (gaai lan). It has a long slender stem topped with small flowering buds that resemble a cross between broccoli florets and an asparagus tip.

Purple broccoli

Purple broccoli tends to have smaller heads with a deep purple tinge, otherwise it is identical to sprouting broccoli.

Chinese broccoli

See Asian greens.

Choose compact bud clusters with no yellowish or large open buds. Heads should be dark green or have a purple tinge (except for Romanesco broccoli – it is a lighter, brighter green).

HOW TO KEEP
Refrigerate in plastic bags. Use promptly.

NUTRITIONAL VALUE
Broccoli is one of the most nutritious vegetables - it is often referred to as the 'nutrition powerhouse'. It's an excellent source of antioxidants, vitamin C, fibre, folate and also supplies calcium, iron, vitamins E and A, and potassium. Broccoli is a rich source of phytochemicals, including glucosinolates, carotenoids, and phenolic compounds. Sulphoraphane, a compound which is formed from broccoli glucosinolates when broccoli is cut or chewed, has been found by scientists to inhibit the development of some cancers. Purple broccoli has even higher levels of vitamin C, folate, iron and calcium and in addition contains anthocyanins, which have antioxidant activity. Broccolini has similar levels of core nutrients to broccoli.

HOW TO PREPARE
Trim the stalks and divide the heads into evenly sized portions. You can eat the stalks – simply leave them attached to the florets. Alternatively the stalks can be removed and cooked separately, slice them finely and use them in stir-fries and soups.
Broccoli is usually eaten cooked – however, the key is to avoid prolonged cooking! In the past the brassica family were often over-cooked. Not only does this taste awful, but it goes mushy or breaks up and many of the nutritional assets are destroyed. Aim for tender and still slightly crisp vegetables – you will find them significantly better in terms of taste, texture and nutrition. Cooking methods such as steaming, microwaving and stir-frying are ideal as they cook foods for a short time in a small amount of water.
Eating brassicas raw in salads, or as coleslaw, or serving them lightly blanched is also an excellent way to maximise their health benefits. To

blanch simply place portions in boiling water for 1–2 minutes, drain and cool under cold running water. Blanching improves taste, colour and texture.

WAYS TO EAT THIS VEGETABLE

Broccoli has many uses – cooked, raw or lightly blanched – the serving possibilities are endless. From salads, pasta dishes, omelettes, quiches, soups to simple accompaniments, broccoli has got to be one of the most versatile vegetables.

AVAILABLE TO PURCHASE

All year round.

TIPS
FOR HOME
GARDENERS

Suitable to plant: spring and summer nationwide. Sow spring and summer. Plant spring, summer.

When to plant: autumn planting is possible in areas with mild winters. Otherwise plant or sow seed from early spring until summer.

Approx time till harvest: three months after sowing or ten weeks after planting.

Depth to plant: 5cm.

Spacing between rows: 30cm.

Spacing between plants: 40cm.

Water requirements: keep watering regularly particularly during dry summer weather.

Gingered greens

Succulent vegetables lightly coated in a ginger and honey sauce taste amazing!

| 6 cups assorted vegetables e.g. cauliflower and broccoli florets, wedges of pepper |
| 1 Tbsp finely chopped fresh ginger |
| 2 Tbsp oil |
| 2 Tbsp honey |
| 2 Tbsp white wine vinegar |

Stir-fry the vegetables and ginger in oil for 8–10 minutes or until tender but still slightly crisp. Add the honey and vinegar and toss well to ensure the vegetables are well coated and the honey has melted. Serve immediately. Serves 4.

Brussels sprouts

A member of the Brassica family, Brussels sprouts look like cute little cabbages. Brussels sprouts are named after the city of Brussels in Belgium from where they are thought to originate.

There are two main Brussels sprouts growing areas in New Zealand. The first is Ohakune, in the Central North Island. It tends to produce smaller hybrid sprouts with compact heads – about 30–45mm. These come to the market earlier in the season and have a higher mustard oil content and hence have a slight piquancy.

The second major growing area is Oamaru in North Otago in the South Island, which tends to produce slightly larger sprouts, 50–60mm, with looser leaves. North Otago Brussels Sprouts (or NOBS) come to the market later in the season and have a sweeter flavour. To cater for the earlier market a hybrid, similar to that coming from Ohakune, also comes from North Otago.

WHAT TO LOOK FOR
It's best to choose Brussels sprouts that are roughly the same size. Avoid yellow, loose, soft or wilting leaves.

HOW TO KEEP
Refrigerate in a plastic bag or crisper.

NUTRITIONAL VALUE
Brussels sprouts are members of the brassica family and are a rich source of phytochemicals, including glucosinolates, carotenoids, and phenolic compounds. They are an excellent source of vitamin C, fibre, folate and a good source of other B group vitamins and vitamin E. They also supply small but significant amounts of calcium, iron, potassium and phosphorus.

HOW TO PREPARE
Remove any loose leaves. Before steaming or boiling cut a cross into the stem end of each sprout to ensure they cook right through.

WAYS TO EAT THIS VEGETABLE
Brussels sprouts are normally served as a side vegetable, either boiled, microwaved or steamed. You can halve them and add to a stir-fry. They can also be used raw and finely sliced in salads, Alternatively lightly blanch them and use whole or halved in salads.

AVAILABLE TO PURCHASE
Hybrids: February – June
North Otago: May – October

Suitable to plant: nationwide.

When to plant: spring and summer in the south, summer and late summer in warmer northern areas.

Approx time till harvest: 3 months.

Depth to plant: 5cm.

Spacing between rows: 60cm.

Spacing between plants: 50cm.

Water requirements: water well during dry weather to prevent a check in plant growth.

Brussels sprouts with hot orange sauce

This hot orange sauce is great over other cooked green vegetables. Try it with broccoli, courgettes, beans or asparagus.

10–12 Brussels sprouts

1 Tbsp margarine

1 Tbsp grated orange rind

¼ cup freshly squeezed orange juice

1 Tbsp sugar

¼ tsp ground ginger

2 Tbsp finely chopped fresh parsley

½ tsp cornflour

Cut a small cross in the base of each sprout. Boil for 5–10 minutes or until softened. Melt the margarine in a separate saucepan. Add all the remaining ingredients, blend well. Heat gently and stir frequently until thickened. Pour the sauce over the drained Brussels sprouts..

Microwave:
Place the Brussels sprouts in a microwave-proof dish, add 2 Tbsp water. Cover and cook on high power for 6–8 minutes. Cook the margarine on high power for 30 seconds. Add the remaining ingredients and cook on high power for 1 minute. Stir well.

Cabbages

Cabbages are one of the oldest vegetables known. Throughout their long history they have often been thought of as food for the poor. There are many varieties of cabbages grown in New Zealand which vary from red, green or white, with smooth or crinkled leaves and round or oval in shape. Taste variations are subtle. As with most vegetables, specific variety names of the brassica group can be confusing as seed companies market similar products with different names.

Green cabbage

These are the most widely grown and available all year round with a range of varieties which ensure a continuous supply. Drumhead is a popular variety with smooth compact leaves. Savoy has crinkly leaves with very good flavour.

Red cabbage

These are hard, tightly packed and crisp with dark red or crimson leaves. Traditionally they are cooked longer than green cabbages. Lemon juice, wine or vinegar must be added to preserve the lovely red colour when cooked. They grow all year round but are more plentiful in autumn and winter.

Cavolonero

Cavolonero means 'black cabbage' in Italian. It is non-hearting with strap-like leaves.

Chinese cabbages

See Asian greens.

Savoy

Drumhead

Red cabbage

HOW TO PREPARE

Sometimes outer leaves are a bit tough. Remove them and any other coarse or damaged leaves. Shred coarsely or finely.

WAYS TO EAT THIS VEGETABLE

Cabbages are delicious either raw or cooked for a short time until tender, but still slightly crisp. Any method of short cooking suits cabbages, especially stir-frying and microwaving. Serve as soon as possible after cooking. Shredded cabbage is the key ingredient of coleslaw, which when teamed with a variety of other ingredients, is a very popular salad. Cabbage leaves, red or green, can be used as a leaf wrapping, stuff with a savoury filling and simmer in liquid until tender. Sauerkraut is a delicious pickled cabbage dish.

AVAILABLE TO PURCHASE

Different varieties of cabbage are available all year round.

TIPS
FOR HOME
GARDENERS

Suitable to plant: nationwide.

When to plant: year round depending on the variety chosen.

Approx time till harvest: 6–8 weeks. Pick when the hearts are firm to the touch.

Depth to plant: 5cm.

Spacing between rows: small varieties 40cm. Large 60cm.

Spacing between plants: 30–60cm depending on variety planted.

Water requirements: water regularly in dry weather, at least once a week.

Citrus coleslaw

Coleslaws are a lot more versatile than you probably think. Like all salads, the fresher the ingredients the better and there are no rules about what should be mixed with what. By trying different ingredients as well as the dressings there are heaps of combinations which you can come up with.

1 orange

3 cups coarsely shredded cabbage

2 spring onions, sliced

½ green pepper, finely chopped

Dressing:

1 Tbsp orange rind

1 Tbsp spiced vinegar

1 Tbsp polyunsaturated oil

1 tsp sugar

freshly ground black pepper

Grate 1 Tbsp of rind from the orange skin to use in the dressing. Peel and slice the orange into rings. Place the orange, cabbage, spring onions and green pepper in a salad bowl. Pour the dressing over the cabbage mixture and mix thoroughly. Serves 4.

Dressing: Blend the orange rind, vinegar, oil, sugar and pepper together.

Capsicum

Capsicums are equally known in New Zealand as peppers or sweet peppers. Native to tropical America, they took several centuries to spread to Europe. It is relatively recently, in the past 30–40 years, that capsicums have been commonly found in New Zealand.

Capsicums are seed pods and can be red, green, yellow, orange, white, purple, brown and lime green. Green and red peppers grow on the same plant, it's just that a red pepper is a ripe green one. Yellow, orange, white and purple are different varieties and are not simply less ripe forms of red or green. Red and green peppers are by far the most commonly found peppers, although yellow and orange peppers are widely available. White, purple, brown and lime green peppers have a more limited supply. Peppers are sweet and juicy with a mild spicy flavour. Being riper, red peppers are sweeter than green peppers. Shape also varies with each variety, from the more commonly found blocky shape to a pointy capsicum. Miniature varieties are sometimes available.

WHAT TO LOOK FOR

Peppers should be well shaped and have skins which are firm and shiny. Avoid those with soft spots or a shrivelled appearance.

HOW TO KEEP

Refrigerate in your vegetable crisper. At some times of the year it is fine to keep capsicums in your fruit bowl.

NUTRITIONAL VALUE

All capsicums are rich in vitamin C and β-carotene; they also supply potassium, folate and other B group vitamins. Red peppers have much higher levels of both vitamin C and carotenoids than immature or yellow or orange types. Immature green peppers have higher levels of flavonoids.

HOW TO PREPARE

You need to remove the seeds and inner membranes. If you want to stuff the capsicum, cut the stem off and remove the seeds from the top, otherwise it's easier to cut the capsicum in half first. If you wish to remove the skins from the peppers, roast, grill or barbecue until the skin blisters and is blackened. Slip the burnt skins off. If they are hard to come off place in a plastic bag or covered dish for a few minutes and then they will be easier to slip off.

WAYS TO EAT THIS VEGETABLE

Peppers are delicious raw or cooked. You can use them raw in a salad, cut them into strips and eat them with dips, or use them as an edible garnish. Peppers taste great in casseroles, on

kebabs, as a side dish, on pizzas, with meat, beans and vegetables and in pasta sauces. Try them stuffed with rice or a bread crumb mixture and baked. Roasted peppers are increasingly popular either hot or cold in salads.

AVAILABLE TO PURCHASE

You can buy peppers all year round but their main season is from January until April.

Greek salad

With flavours and textures as fresh and crisp as these it is not hard to see why this salad has become such a classic.

2 Tbsp white wine vinegar
2 Tbsp olive oil
1 tsp sugar
½ telegraph cucumber, diced
½ red pepper, diced
½ green pepper, diced
½ yellow pepper, diced
2 tomatoes, diced
1 red skinned onion, diced
¼ cup feta cheese, diced (50g)
⅓ cup black olives

Blend the vinegar, oil and sugar together. Pour over the rest of the ingredients and mix well.

TIPS
FOR HOME
GARDENERS

Suitable to plant: warm frost-free areas.

When to plant: spring and summer in frost-free areas.

Approx time till harvest: three months.

Depth to plant: 5cm.

Spacing between rows: 50cm.

Spacing between plants: 40–50cm.

Water requirements: water regularly in summer. Liquid fertiliser applied fortnightly will boost the crop.

Carrots

Carrots have been a staple in many countries for thousands of years although it is only since the 16th century that they have been orange. Earliest records show carrots were purple; later records show red, yellow and white carrots were found. It is interesting that some seed companies are now introducing a rainbow of multi-coloured carrots and marketing them as new varieties!

Different varieties of carrots have subtle taste variations and slightly different shaped tapers.

WHAT TO LOOK FOR

Choose carrots that are firm, well formed and have a good orange colour. Smaller carrots tend to be sweeter and more tender. Spring carrots sold with the leaves attached should have leaves which are fresh and bright green.

HOW TO KEEP

Provided they are stored correctly, carrots continue to provide good levels of nutrition for a reasonably long period of time. Refrigerate in plastic bags. Peeled baby carrots are actually larger carrots which are trimmed down to 'baby size' for sale. They will keep for at least a week in the fridge. As they're already peeled, a light frosting may appear on the surface. Just soak in cold water for a while and they'll return to their brilliant orange colour.

NUTRITIONAL VALUE

Carrots are an excellent source of vitamin A, through α-carotene and β-carotene which are converted to vitamin A by the body. Another important phytochemical present is falcarinol and it may be responsible for some of the health benefits of carrots. Falcarinol is a substance of recent nutritional interest and one that is also present in ginseng which is a long established Chinese health remedy. One medium-sized carrot supplies enough β-carotene for two days' supply of vitamin A. Moderate amounts of vitamin C, sodium, potassium and fibre are also present. B group vitamins are also present in small but useful amounts.

HOW TO PREPARE

Young carrots don't need peeling. Simply wash well or lightly scrape to ensure all soil is removed. Only old and large carrots need to be peeled. Carrots are versatile in both preparation and cooking methods. Either cut into rings, cubes, strips, or chunks.
Carrots are often grated for salads. Vary the size of your grater and experiment with some of the more interesting coarse graters or peelers.

WAYS TO EAT THIS VEGETABLE

They can be eaten raw or cooked and are found in savoury and some sweet dishes, such as carrot cake or muffins. They can be boiled, steamed, baked, roasted, barbecued, stir-fried or microwaved. Carrots should be cooked until they're tender and depending on preference, still slightly crunchy. Cooked tender carrots may be mashed or puréed. Cooking for a short time over a high heat in a little oil, e.g. stir-frying, is probably the best way to maximise nutritional benefits.

AVAILABLE TO PURCHASE

All year round. Spring carrots are available mainly in the spring and summer months.

TIPS
FOR HOME
GARDENERS

Suitable to plant: suitable for growing throughout the country.

When to plant: as plants resent frost they are best sown in spring when the soil has warmed.

Approx time till harvest: 8–10 weeks.

Depth to plant: sow seed shallowly a few cm deep.

Spacing between rows: 20cm.

Spacing between plants: thin seedlings once they have sprouted and allow a few cm between each maturing plant.

Water requirements: sow seed in a sunny position in a moist yet well drained soil.

Carrots with lemon

Glazing vegetables with a slightly sweet citrus sauce is stunning. Using the microwave makes it very quick and easy – the automatic function on most microwaves takes away any guesswork ensuring they are cooked to perfection every time.

3 medium carrots (400g), peeled and cut into rings

1 Tbsp brown sugar

1 Tbsp butter

1 tsp grated lemon rind

2 Tbsp lemon juice

freshly ground black pepper

2 Tbsp finely chopped fresh coriander

Place the carrot pieces, brown sugar, butter, rind, juice and pepper in a microwave-proof dish. Mix, cover and cook on high power for 4–6 minutes or until tender. Stir once during cooking. Mix the coriander through the carrots. Serves 4.

Cauliflower

Cauliflower, from the Latin word meaning 'cabbage flower', is a member of the Brassica family. It has been grown for more than 2000 years. Native to the Mediterranean, it has been part of the European diet for about 500 years. It is now a popular vegetable in New Zealand. Miniature cauliflowers, ideal for a single serve, are sometimes available.

Broccoflower

A hybrid mix of cauliflower and broccoli. The florets are bright green (lighter than broccoli) and packed into a round head like cauliflower. The flavour tends to be sweeter than cauliflower and broccoli. Supply is limited.

WHAT TO LOOK FOR

Checking the colour and freshness of the leaves that are close to the head (known as curds) is a good way of helping choose the best cauliflower. Look for white heads that are clean and compact. The curds should be firm with no parts breaking away.

HOW TO KEEP

Refrigerate in plastic bags.

NUTRITIONAL VALUE

Cauliflower is an excellent source of vitamin C and supplies vitamin K and folate. It is also a source of fibre and other B group vitamins as well as small amounts of potassium and calcium. Cauliflower is a member of the brassica family of vegetables and hence is a rich source of many phytochemicals, particularly the flavonoids and glucosinolates.

HOW TO PREPARE

Cut into florets or leave whole. Cauliflower is best cooked for a short time until tender but still slightly crisp. Avoid overcooking as the taste will be inferior and the heads will disintegrate. To lightly cook cauliflower florets for use in salads or crudités, simply place in boiling water for 2–3 minutes, drain and cool under cold running water.

WAYS TO EAT THIS VEGETABLE

Cauliflower tastes delicious raw or lightly steamed, boiled or stir-fried. Use cauliflower like broccoli. They're good eaten together. Cauliflower is great with a cheese or white sauce, added raw or lightly cooked to salads, made into pickles, added to soups, casseroles and stir-fries. It's also good for using as crudités, either raw or blanched, served with dip or dipping sauce.

AVAILABLE TO PURCHASE

All year round.

Cauliflower cheese

2 cups dry macaroni

¼ small cauliflower (200g)

½ head broccoli (200g)

2 Tbsp butter or margarine

1 onion, finely chopped

3 Tbsp flour

3 cups milk

2 cups grated tasty cheese

1 tomato, sliced

¼ cup crushed weetbix

2 carrots, cut into sticks

2 celery stalks, cut into sticks

Fill a large saucepan with water, bring to the boil, add the macaroni and simmer for 7 minutes. Chop the cauliflower and broccoli into florets. Add to the pasta and simmer another 3–4 minutes. Drain. Meanwhile melt the butter in a saucepan. Sauté the onion for 3–4 minutes. Add the flour, mix well and gradually add the milk. Heat gently until thickened, stirring to avoid lumps. Add the cheese. Place the macaroni vegetable mix in a baking dish, pour over the cheese sauce. Top with the tomatoes and sprinkle the weetbix over. Grill for 5–10 minutes or until golden brown. Serve with celery and carrot sticks.

TIPS FOR HOME GARDENERS

Suitable to plant: nationwide.

When to plant: depending on the variety chosen cauliflower can be sown and grown year round.

Approx time till harvest: 3 months.

Depth to plant: plant 5–8cm.

Spacing between rows: small varieties 30cm, large 50cm.

Spacing between plants: small 25cm, large 40–50cm.

Water requirements: water frequently when growing. Once heads start to form avoid watering the foliage.

WHAT TO LOOK FOR

Look for bunches with a good tight formation. Leaves should be fresh and unwilted. Stems should be firm and crisp when snapped. Brown or cracked bunches should be avoided.

HOW TO KEEP

Refrigerate in a plastic bag. Alternatively, refrigerate with the butt end in 2–3cm of water; change water daily.

NUTRITIONAL VALUE

The core nutrients in celery are vitamin C, sodium, potassium, calcium, fibre, and a small amount of vitamin A as β-carotene. Antioxidants include carotenoids and flavonoids.

HOW TO PREPARE

Stalks and leaves can be eaten raw or cooked. Remove strings from coarse stalks. This won't be necessary if the stalks are young.

WAYS TO EAT THIS VEGETABLE

Sliced and lightly stir-fried celery makes a good side vegetable by itself, especially when drizzled with sesame oil and sesame seeds. Alternatively celery

Celery

Celery, as we know it today, is very much an Italian vegetable. It was in Italy in the Middle Ages that it was first used as food. White celery, which farmers grew away from the sunlight, was the most common variety and in Europe it is still popular.

New Zealanders used to prefer white celery too – until green-stemmed celery was developed in the United States in the 1940s and was successfully introduced into New Zealand in the 1960s. Nowadays we prefer our celery bright green. Varieties are now available with little or no stringiness.

teams well with many other vegetables as a side vegetable. Add celery to all sorts of savoury dishes like casseroles, pies or soups. The leaves can be used in salads, soups, stocks, casseroles or as a garnish.

Celery is also great raw in salads or as a snack. A perennial favourite with children is celery sticks filled with crunchy peanut butter. Fresh young celery leaves from the centre of the bunch are great mixed with other leaves in a green salad.

AVAILABLE TO PURCHASE
All year round.

TIPS
FOR HOME
GARDENERS

Suitable to plant: nationwide.

When to plant: spring and summer.

Approx time till harvest: germination of seed can be slow. Seedlings will also take several months to mature.

Depth to plant: plant deeply at approx 10cm.

Spacing between rows: 50cm.

Spacing between plants: 30cm.

Water requirements: provide with generous quantities of water throughout the growing season.

Herbed greens

Stir-frying captures the flavours brilliantly. The trick is not to overcook the cabbage and that you serve it as soon as it is cooked. So simple – and so delicious.

6 cups shredded cabbage and sliced celery

2 Tbsp oil

2 Tbsp fresh herbs, finely chopped

1 or 2 cloves crushed garlic

2 Tbsp honey

2 Tbsp white wine vinegar

Stir-fry the vegetables and garlic in oil for 4–5 minutes or until tender but still slightly crisp. Add the herbs, honey and vinegar and toss well to ensure the vegetables are well coated and the honey has melted. Serve immediately. Serves 4.

Chilli peppers

Chilli peppers are related to the sweet pepper. There are literally hundreds of varieties of chilli peppers. Some are definitely more suited to particular end uses than others. If using them raw it is essential to select a variety which doesn't have a tough skin. It is quite normal for many chillies to change colour as they ripen and the colour transition is often green to black/brown to red. The intensity of the heat also increases as the chilli ripens.

Although all chilli peppers are hot, some are hotter than others. As a general rule, the smaller the pepper, the darker the colour, the more pointed the top and narrower the shoulders, the hotter it will be – although there are quite a few exceptions! Chillies are rated according to their relative heat.

To alleviate the effects of really hot chillies use yoghurt or cucumber.

A Dutch red
This chilli looks very attractive but has a rather leathery texture. It is best dried, plaited and used in sauces or curry pastes.

B New Mexican
Anaheim is a mild flavoured, large chilli pepper which naturally ripens green to black/brown to red. It is quite often stuffed when green or black/brown. When red it is often used for decorative purposes or used in sauces or pastes.

C Wax
The Hungarian yellow wax is a very attractive large long chilli. It is very mild and is picked when a green/yellow colour. It is ideal to use raw in salads, added to stir-fries or it can be pickled. If left to ripen it goes orange and becomes very hot. A banana chilli is similar to this.

D Jalapeno
Jalapeno chillies are cylindrical in shape with a blunt point and are available in green and red. Green jalapeno is most commonly used raw, sliced on nachos or in a salsa. Red jalapeno has tough skin and is best not used raw but rather in sauces, pickles or dried.

E South American yellow
A very attractive medium sized, dark yellow chilli pepper which is good used raw or cooked. It ranges in taste from medium sweet, ideal for use with chicken, to hot, which is particularly good in meat dishes.

F Cayenne peppers
The two most commonly found in New Zealand are the Asian cayenne pepper which is green and the Mexican pepper which is red. Both of these are ideal used in chilli and curry pastes, and the red is good in sauces. The skins, which are often quite thick, are too tough when raw.

G Exotics
Thai or bird's eye chillies are preferred in many Asian dishes and tend to be rather hot. They are a small long thin chilli and are available either red or green. They are very versatile and may be used either raw or cooked.

Haberno (Scotch bonnet)
This is a Mexican chilli which is a very attractive, lantern shaped, light green to orange coloured pod. It is extremely hot with an aromatic fruity flavour. Haberno is said to be the hottest chilli grown commercially.

WHAT TO LOOK FOR

Chilli peppers should be well shaped and have skins which are firm and shiny. Avoid those with soft spots or a shrivelled appearance.

NUTRITIONAL VALUE

For most people chillies are eaten only in small quantities so are more important for their taste than their nutritional value.

HOW TO KEEP

Chillies do not need to be refrigerated and will stay firm at room temperature for 3–4 weeks. They may begin to dry out and this is still quite acceptable for use. Chillies freeze well and may be used straight from the freezer; do not thaw.

HOW TO PREPARE

Chilli peppers are usually chopped very finely. After handling the chillies, don't touch your eyes, nose or mouth until you've washed your hands. To ascertain the chilli's 'temperature', first touch the tip of your tongue on the pepper and wait one minute. If a burning sensation develops, consider the chilli 'very hot'. If you feel nothing, cut off a tiny piece and nibble. You can label medium or mild, and use quantities accordingly. It is better to be cautious and begin by adding small quantities – you can always add more!

WAYS TO EAT THIS VEGETABLE

Chilli peppers are the key flavouring ingredient in a lot of Mexican, Spanish, Indian, Asian, and especially Thai, dishes.

AVAILABLE TO PURCHASE

You can buy chillies all year round but their main season is from January until April.

TIPS
FOR HOME
GARDENERS

Suitable to plant: warm sunny areas.

When to plant: spring and summer.

Approx time till harvest: 4 months.

Depth to plant: 10cm.

Spacing between rows: 50cm.

Spacing between plants: 40–50cm.

Water requirements: supply with regular quantities of water throughout the growing period.

Guacamole

Always popular and so easy!

1–2 ripe avocados, peeled and mashed

1 Tbsp red chilli peppers, finely chopped

2 tomatoes, finely chopped

1 Tbsp lemon juice

1 small mild or red onion, peeled and finely chopped

freshly ground black pepper

Blend the avocado, chillies, tomatoes, lemon juice, onion and pepper together. Serve with fresh vegetable sticks, with corn chips, or on fresh crusty bread.

Celeriac

Celeriac is a type of celery, well known in England, Europe, Asia and India. It has a unique flavour and is very refreshing even when raw. The short stem and upper part of the roots grow into a cream-green coloured round shape about 10–15cm in diameter. The skin is textured and ridged. The flesh is creamy-white and firm but not as firm in texture as carrots.

Celeriac and parsnip mash

600g celeriac, peeled to remove all the knobbly skin and cut into chunks

2 parsnips, peeled and cut into chunks

2 tsp wholegrain mustard

2–3 Tbsp trim milk

1 Tbsp butter

freshly ground black pepper

Boil celeriac and parsnip for 25–35 minutes or until soft. Drain. Add the mustard, milk and butter. Roughly mash, leaving small chunks of the different vegetables within the mix. Season generously with pepper. Serves 4.

WHAT TO LOOK FOR
Select smaller roots, as they are more tender.

HOW TO KEEP
Refrigerate in your crisper or in a plastic bag.

NUTRITIONAL VALUE
Celeriac is a good source of fibre, supplying around three times as much as regular celery. It is a good source of vitamin C, folate and small amounts of other vitamins and minerals including potassium, iron and calcium.

HOW TO PREPARE
To prepare celeriac, peel and cut into slices. The stalk and the leaves are not used as they are bitter and stringy.

WAYS TO EAT THIS VEGETABLE
Celeriac can be used either raw or lightly cooked in salads. Cook until soft and tender either by microwaving, boiling, steaming or stir-frying. Celeriac is often mashed and served as a side vegetable. It can also be fried into chips or brushed with olive oil and baked in the oven.

AVAILABLE TO PURCHASE
Celeriac is available from autumn through to early spring.

TIPS FOR HOME GARDENERS

Suitable to plant: nationwide.

When to plant: spring and summer.

Approx time till harvest: 8–10 weeks.

Depth to plant: 5cm.

Spacing between rows: 30cm.

Spacing between plants: 20cm.

Water requirements: celeriac, the turnip-rooted celery, grows best if it has regular quantities of water and a rich soil.

Chokos

Chokos are a native of Central America. They were taken back to Europe by the Spanish explorers and from there were introduced to parts of Asia. Choko is also known as chayote, vegetable pear or mango squash. They grow on a climbing plant and look a bit like a pear. Some varieties have spines, others are spineless. Colours range from green to ivory white. They have a very mild flavour, often likened to that of marrow, so are usually cooked with other stronger tasting foods. Choko shoots are sometimes eaten in Asian cooking.

Choko fruit curry

Although it's hard to beat the succulence of choko in this fragrant and rather exotic curry, marrow, courgettes, egg plant, kumara, potato and pumpkin all work well.

2 choko, (300–400g) peeled and chopped into bite-sized pieces	¼ cup sultanas
1 onion, peeled and chopped	1 Tbsp desiccated coconut
1 carrot, chopped	¼ cup chutney
1 apple, chopped	1 cup water
6 dried apricots, chopped	1 tsp mild curry powder or paste

Place all ingredients in a saucepan. Cover and simmer for 20 minutes or until the carrot is soft. Serve garnished with a spoonful of yoghurt and/or extra coconut, accompanied by rice and/or poppadoms. If you like a creamy curry, gently stir in ½ cup yoghurt just before serving. Serves 4.

WHAT TO LOOK FOR
Look for firm, even-coloured chokos which are about 10–15cm long and are not too deeply wrinkled. Sometimes smaller chokos, around 5cm long are used as well. Large whiter coloured chokos indicate older fruit.

HOW TO KEEP
Refrigerate in plastic bags and they will keep for a few weeks.

NUTRITIONAL VALUE
Chokos are a source of vitamin C.

HOW TO PREPARE
Large chokos need to be peeled before cooking. Cut the choko in half and remove the seeds. Some people eat the seeds which have have a nutty flavour. If boiling or steaming, leave the skin on to retain the flavour, cook for about 15–20 minutes or until tender. Small chokos, under 5cm, don't need to be peeled and are perfect for stir-fries.

WAYS TO EAT THIS VEGETABLE
Choko halves can be stuffed with all sorts of fillings – rice, bacon, tomato, onion, cheese and more. They can be used much like courgettes. Having a mild flavour they go particularly well with flavours like pesto, ginger, garlic and tomatoes. They can be served with a sauce, added to casseroles and stir-fries and even used in desserts, tarts, breads, jams or cakes.

AVAILABLE TO PURCHASE
April to June; availability is sometimes limited.

TIPS
FOR HOME
GARDENERS

Suitable to plant: warm sheltered sub-tropical areas only.

When to plant: spring.

Approx time till harvest: in the first year a few fruit can be expected and crops increase year after year.

Depth to plant and spacing: plant the tuber-like fruit 9cm below the soil surface. A single vine will climb on sheds and fences and cover many metres. One vine is probably sufficient for most.

Water requirements: plants are hardy, however for good fruit development give ample water in dry summer weather.

Courgettes or zucchini

Usually green-skinned but yellow-skinned varieties are also available. Courgettes are at their best when about 16–20cm long. Courgettes grow on the plant behind a yellow flower. If they are picked early the flower may be still attached. Rarely seen for sale because they are so difficult to transport, the flowers attached to the courgette are highly prized. They are often stuffed with a creamy ricotta-based filling and baked still attached to the courgette. Home gardeners can pick them with the flower still attached.

Marrows

Marrows have a coarser texture and lesser flavour than courgettes. Unlike courgettes, you do need to peel marrows and remove the seeds. Marrows may be steamed, baked, boiled or fried. Baked stuffed marrows are particularly delicious. Cut them in half, do not peel, scoop out the centre and stuff with a savoury filling before baking.

Scallopini

Small and spherical and usually a lighter green than marrows and courgettes. Dark green and yellow varieties are also available. Scallopini are prepared in the same way as courgettes. The shape of the scallopini makes them particularly appealing.

Courgettes, marrow & scallopini

Courgettes originated in Italy and were popular in the Mediterranean region hundreds of years before they became popular in the Western world. These are all members of the summer squash family. Courgette is the French name, zucchini the Italian name; in New Zealand we use both names interchangeably. Some people also refer to them as baby marrows, which indeed they are. Marrows are simply mature or big courgettes.

WHAT TO LOOK FOR

Choose summer squash that have glossy blemish-free skins. Avoid any that show signs of softening or withering.

HOW TO KEEP

Refrigerate in plastic bags. Use promptly.

NUTRITIONAL VALUE

Courgettes are an excellent source of vitamin C and also supply folate, potassium and some fibre and small amounts of other vitamins and minerals.

HOW TO PREPARE

Courgettes and scallopini are very versatile and easy to prepare. Simply trim the stalk end off and eat either raw or cooked. There is no need to peel them.

WAYS TO EAT THIS VEGETABLE

Steam, boil, microwave, bake, stir-fry, barbecue or grill courgettes or scallopini as a side vegetable. They are particularly good in stir-fries and barbecues or filled with a savoury stuffing and baked. They are good when used raw in salads. Courgettes can also be grated or finely chopped and used in flans or quiches. In a similar manner to carrots they also make delicious moist cakes and breads.

AVAILABLE TO PURCHASE

They are available all year round with the main growing season from October until May.

TIPS
FOR HOME
GARDENERS

Suitable to plant: warm sheltered gardens nationwide.

When to plant: summer.

Approx time till harvest: 4–6 weeks.

Depth to plant: 6cm.

Spacing between rows: 60cm–2m depending on the variety.

Spacing between plants: 60cm–2m.

Water requirements: water well when the fruit are forming.

Garlic greens

Stir-frying captures the flavours of vegetables brilliantly. Begin by cooking denser vegetables (those that take longer to cook e.g. broccoli or celery) and add less dense vegetables towards the end of the cooking time (e.g. leafy ones). If the pan starts to dry out just add a sprinkling of water to keep it nice and moist. The vegetables used in this recipe are interchangeable – use whatever is in season or try new ones.

6 cups assorted green vegetables (e.g. sliced courgettes, leeks, asparagus, beans etc)

3–4 cloves garlic, finely chopped

2 Tbsp oil

2 Tbsp honey

2 Tbsp white wine vinegar

Stir-fry the vegetables and garlic in oil for 8–10 minutes or until tender but still slightly crisp. Add the honey and vinegar and toss well to ensure the vegetables are well coated and the honey has melted. Serve immediately. Serves 4.

Cucumber

Cucumbers are thought to have originated in Southern Asia and were very popular in India. They eventually spread to Europe, where for thousands of years they were used to quench thirst. Related to the watermelon and with a water content of 96%, it is easy to see why they are so refreshing. Cucumbers are very popular in summery salads, adding an interesting texture. In New Zealand we can buy several varieties of cucumber.

Telegraph cucumber

This is the most popular cucumber and is grown under glass. It is long, usually about 30–45cm, and is often individually wrapped in plastic. This is because it has a very soft skin that is easily damaged. The plastic also stops it drying out and going soft. Telegraph cucumbers are often referred to as seedless as, when harvested at their best, the seeds are immature or virtually nonexistent.

Short cucumber

You'll sometimes hear this called the standard or stubby cucumber. It is short and has a slightly uneven surface. Grown indoors all year round, it can also be grown outdoors in the summer. The skin on a standard cucumber is tougher than a telegraph cucumber and is often peeled. For some uses the seeds are also removed.

Lebanese cucumber

A recent addition to the market in New Zealand, the Lebanese cucumber is green skinned and white fleshed and is relatively small at around 12–15cm long. It has a tender skin which does not need to be peeled, a very sweet taste and a very juicy texture.

Apple cucumber

This is a pale yellow cucumber with a diameter of around 9cm and is about 12cm long. It is crisp like an apple and has a very mild sweet flavour. The skin can be quite hard so it is usually peeled.

Gherkin

This is very small, between 5–10cm long, and is grown only for pickling.

WHAT TO LOOK FOR

The best cucumbers will have a firm skin and an even colour. The shade of the cucumber is important with telegraph and short cucumbers; a vibrant green colour assures the buyer that the cucumbers have recently come from the vine, whilst a dull green or yellow indicates age.

HOW TO KEEP

Store them in the warmest part of the fridge as storing at lower temperatures will cause chilling damage, and use promptly. At cooler times of the year it is alright to store them on the bench. Lebanese cucumbers are always best refrigerated.

NUTRITIONAL VALUE

Cucumbers are relatively poor in terms of nutrient content, however they are one of only a few foods to contain silicon. Silicon isn't a very common mineral and some sources state that it is important in connective tissue such as skin, hair and nails. Eating both the skin and seeds will deliver the best nutritional benefits. Cucumbers also contain some vitamin C, provitamin A as β-carotene in the skins, fibre through their skin and seeds, and potassium. Lebanese cucumbers have about twice as much vitamin C as other varieties.

Short Cucumber

Lebanese

Gherkin

HOW TO PREPARE

Young cucumbers have a mild and tender skin and it is unnecessary to peel them. Telegraph cucumbers never need to be peeled. Many European recipe books advocate peeling and removing the seeds, but in New Zealand the whole cucumber is usually enjoyed.

WAYS TO EAT THIS VEGETABLE

Cucumbers are most popular as a salad vegetable, but they can be prepared in a surprising number of other ways. They make an excellent cold soup. They can also be peeled and chopped and then sautéed to serve with fish. Cucumbers can be hollowed out and filled with a savoury filling which depending on the type of filling may be either eaten raw, microwaved or baked. Cucumber is a great addition to pickles or chutneys. Slices of cucumber with a topping such as salmon or paté can be used as you would crackers when serving nibbles with drinks.

AVAILABLE TO PURCHASE

Available all year round. Short and apple cucumbers are most plentiful in the summer months.

TIPS
FOR HOME
GARDENERS

Suitable to plant: warm, sheltered gardens nationwide.

When to plant: late spring, early summer.

Approx time till harvest: 6–8 weeks.

Depth to plant: 5cm.

Spacing between rows: 1m.

Spacing between plants: 40–50cm.

Water requirements: moist well-drained soil suits them best. Ensure a free flow of air around plants.

Tomato, basil and cucumber salad

1 telegraph cucumber, sliced into ribbons

5 tomatoes cut into chunky slices

1 bunch fresh basil

2–3 Tbsp balsamic vinaigrette

Toss together and drizzle with the balsamic vinaigrette. Serves 4.

Egg plant

Also known as the aubergine, egg plant is very common in Southern European countries where it is highly prized. The Greek put egg plant in a traditional recipe called moussaka, the French in their traditional recipe, ratatouille, and the Turks in imam bayildi. Actually a fruit, egg plants contain many fine seeds. They have a mild taste and are typically cooked with stronger flavours such as garlic, tomatoes, onions, herbs and spices.

Several varieties of egg plant are available in New Zealand. Skin colours range from a deep purple, almost black, to a light purple with creamy streaks, to all white. Even a green-yellow 'banana' egg plant and small Thai green egg plants no larger than marbles can sometimes be found. Shapes are also variable, from the more commonly found pear-shape to long and thin cylindrical shapes. Growing conditions can affect the colouring, for instance a white egg plant may be all white if grown indoors but would have purple streaks if grown outdoors. By far the most commonly found variety is the deep purple pear-shaped egg plant.

The large white egg plant, which (interestingly enough) is about the size of a mandarine and is the very small white egg plant illustrated above, can be eaten raw and is often served as a side dish with Thai meals. It tastes similar to beans. The Japanese egg plant, the long thin purple one, also tastes similar to a bean and is often stir-fried with oyster sauce.

WHAT TO LOOK FOR

Look for glossy blemish-free skin which is firm to the touch and shows no signs of withering. Decay appears as dark brown spots on the surface and should be avoided as these egg plants will deteriorate rapidly. Egg plants should be heavy in relation to size.

HOW TO KEEP

Refrigerate in the crisper.

NUTRITIONAL VALUE

Whilst egg plant is not rich in core nutrients, it can contain unusual pigments and has high levels of other phytochemicals, particularly phenolic compounds like nasunin, which are thought to confer much of its high levels of antioxidant activity.

HOW TO PREPARE

Egg plants are normally used unpeeled. Remove the calyx. Some recipes will instruct slicing the egg plant, sprinkling with salt and leaving for 30 minutes before rinsing thoroughly. This is to drain out any bitterness, but as only very ripe egg plants tend to be bitter, this isn't usually necessary. Recently developed varieties are not bitter. Some egg plants, particularly the smaller ones, are so tender they can be eaten raw.

WAYS TO EAT THIS VEGETABLE

Egg plants can be fried, baked, grilled or steamed - whole, sliced or cubed. They go well with lamb and chicken and can be cut into chunks and barbecued on kebabs. They're great stuffed with other vegetables and meats. Many countries have traditional egg plant recipes, e.g. moussaka, ratatouille and imam bayildi.

AVAILABLE TO PURCHASE

Purple varieties are available all year round with most plentiful quantities from November until June. Other varieties have a more limited supply.

TIPS
FOR HOME
GARDENERS

Suitable to plant: warm sheltered gardens only.

When to plant: spring.

Approx time till harvest: 10–12 weeks.

Depth to plant: 5cm.

Spacing between rows: 30cm.

Spacing between plants: 30cm.

Water requirements: drought tolerant, however they grow best in a sunny position in well-drained soil.

Moussaka

This classic Middle Eastern dish is an excellent recipe to start with if you have not tried egg plant before. However don't discount this wonderful recipe if you don't have egg plant. *It is also delicious with courgette, marrow, potato…or lashings of spinach or silver beet. The white stalks of the silver beet are fabulous as the base.

1–2 Tbsp oil
1 large egg plant (500g) in 1cm slices *or enough of any of the vegetables above to provide a generous layer in your chosen dish(es)
400g minced lamb or beef
2 onions, peeled and diced
2 cloves crushed garlic
1 capsicum, chopped
500ml pasta sauce

½ tsp ground allspice
1 cup breadcrumbs
1 cup grated cheese
White sauce
½ cup skim milk powder
¼ cup plain flour
½ tsp ground or freshly grated nutmeg
1 cup boiling water
1 egg

Warm the oil in a heavy based pan, cook the egg plant slices until golden brown. Arrange in the base of a greased ovenproof dish, or individual ramekins.

Add more oil to pan if necessary. Brown mince, add the onions, garlic and capsicum, cook for 5 minutes until vegetables are beginning to brown. Add pasta sauce and all spice, cover and simmer, stirring occasionally for 20 minutes or until the meat is tender and nearly all the liquid has evaporated.

Meanwhile assemble the white sauce: Place milk powder, flour, nutmeg and freshly boiled water in a heatproof bowl and beat well until smooth and creamy. Add egg and beat again.

Combine the breadcrumbs and cheese, sprinkle half over the egg plant. Spoon meat sauce over, then the white sauce. Sprinkle with remaining cheese and breadcrumb mixture. Bake at 180°C for 20–30 minutes or until golden brown on top. The moussaka will 'set' during baking, making it easy to cut and serve.

Fennel

Fennel, sometimes known as Florence fennel, has a long history and is one of the oldest cultivated plants. Roman warriors used to eat fennel to keep them in good health while Roman women ate it to prevent obesity. The leaves are often used as a herb. The characteristic aniseed flavour and aroma make it a delightful vegetable which, although not widely eaten in New Zealand, is very popular in many other countries. Miniature varieties are sometimes available.

Fennel soup

3 fennel bulbs	1 large onion, coarsely chopped
1 Tbsp olive oil	1L vegetable stock
3 medium potatoes, peeled and diced	salt and pepper to taste

Trim fennel bulbs, quarter and chop. Keep tips and leaves for garnishing. Heat oil in a large saucepan. Add the fennel, potatoes and onion and sauté for 5 minutes. Add the stock and stir well. Bring to the boil, reduce heat, cover and simmer for 30 minutes. Remove from heat and season with salt and pepper. Garnish with the fennel tips and leaves. Serves 4–6.

WHAT TO LOOK FOR
Select firm plump white bulbs with fresh feathery foliage. Small bulbs which are less than 12cm in diameter are more tender.

HOW TO KEEP
Refrigerate in the crisper and use as soon as possible.

NUTRITIONAL VALUE
Fennel is a good source of vitamin C.

HOW TO PREPARE
Cut off the base and stalks, retain any foliage for garnish. Every part of the plant from seed to the root is edible. If boiling, use as little water as possible to retain the flavour.

WAYS TO EAT THIS VEGETABLE
Add finely sliced or grated raw or cooked stems to salads or sandwiches. Steam, microwave, stir-fry or boil the bulb to serve as a side vegetable. Roast fennel in a little olive oil with garlic, lemon juice and a sprinkling of brown sugar is fantastic. Fennel is particularly delicious with a light cheese sauce or when cooked in a tomato-based sauce or with chicken or meat stock. Fennel leaf can be used as a substitute for dill and is an excellent flavouring herb with many vegetables, particularly courgettes, carrots, beans and cabbage.

AVAILABLE TO PURCHASE
Fennel is available in limited quantities in the autumn and winter months.

TIPS
FOR HOME
GARDENERS

Suitable to plant: nationwide.

When to plant: depending on the variety chosen, spring or autumn.

Approx time till harvest: 4 weeks.

Depth to plant: 5cm.

Spacing between rows: 40cm.

Spacing between plants: 20cm.

Water requirements: a moist fertile soil is best, however plants are drought tolerant.

Ginger

Ginger originated in southern provinces of China and India where it has been used in food and medicines for over 5000 years. Fresh ginger is a key flavour used in many Asian cuisines and has become very popular in New Zealand. It is a root crop which has a pungent spicy aroma and characteristic taste.

Myoga ginger

Myoga ginger is a traditional Japanese vegetable grown for both the shoots and flower buds. Freshly sliced myoga shoots and buds are commonly used in salads and miso soup. The shoots are also preserved whole in vinegar as an edible garnish. This is a new vegetable in New Zealand and research is still being undertaken on growth and yield.

WHAT TO LOOK FOR
Select plump, heavy, smooth roots which are free from spots and wrinkles.

HOW TO KEEP
Keep in a cool dry place away from the sunlight.

NUTRITIONAL VALUE
For most people ginger is eaten only in small quantities so is more important for its great taste than nutritional value.

HOW TO PREPARE
Ginger is generally peeled and is then finely chopped, sliced or grated.

WAYS TO EAT THIS VEGETABLE
Ginger provides a wonderful flavour for stir-fries, salads, soups and marinades, and is a good accompanying flavour for pork, beef, chicken and fish.

AVAILABLE TO PURCHASE
Imported ginger is available all year round.

Marinated vegetable salad

These tender, but slightly crisp, vegetables marinated in a subtle ginger dressing taste sensational. Make this salad a few hours before you need it to allow the flavours to mingle.

1 green pepper, cut into chunks	½ cup wine vinegar
1 large carrot, cut into thin sticks	½ cup sugar
4–6 Brussels sprouts, halved	½ cup boiling water
1 cup cauliflower florets	2cm piece root ginger, peeled and thinly sliced
1 cup broccoli florets	
3 spring onions, cut into 4cm lengths	dash of tabasco sauce (optional)

Blanch the vegetables in boiling water for 2–3 minutes. Cool under cold running water. Mix the vinegar, sugar, water, ginger and tabasco sauce until the sugar dissolves. Cool and pour over the vegetables. Allow to marinate for 3–4 hours.

TIPS
FOR HOME
GARDENERS

Suitable to plant: hot sheltered gardens only.

When to plant: spring and summer.

Approx time till harvest: 8–10 weeks.

Depth to plant: 10cm.

Spacing between rows: 40cm.

Spacing between plants: 40cm.

Water requirements: regular quantities of water are essential during dry weather.

Garlic

Garlic is a member of the onion family which also includes onions, of course, and chives, shallots, spring onions and leeks. Throughout history garlic has been the topic of many old wives' tales and folklores, from keeping vampires away to curing toothache if held in the palm of your hand! Garlic has long been recorded as having cured this and that. There is some truth in this, as recent research has shown that the entire onion family, particularly garlic, does have some properties that destroy bacteria and protect against heart disease.

Garlic has been cultivated in Central Asia for thousands of years. As early as 2000 BC, the Chinese were using it in their cooking. Garlic is now used world-wide. The most common varieties of garlic contain 10 cloves (or segments) with white skin on them. Other varieties have pink or purple skin and larger cloves. As a rule, the smaller the clove, the stronger the taste.

WHAT TO LOOK FOR

Look for firm well shaped cloves. Buy in small amounts and break off only the cloves you are going to use immediately. Garlic dries out once detached. To tell if the garlic is New Zealand grown, check for roots. Each New Zealand grown bulb of garlic has had its roots trimmed, one at a time. If a bulb is bald, that is, it has no roots, it is imported!

HOW TO KEEP

Keep in a cool dry place away from the sunlight. Don't put in a plastic bag or store in the fridge – or everything in your fridge will end up tasting of garlic!

NUTRITIONAL VALUE

For most people garlic is eaten only in small quantities so is more important for its great taste than nutritional value. However as the potent powers of garlic are being realised many people are deciding to eat more! Garlic is a concentrated mixture of phytochemicals, which are likely to interact and have synergistic effects. The major phytochemicals are sulphur-containing compounds and saponins. Some flavonoids are also present. Garlic also supplies vitamins, particularly vitamin C and B6. There is also an assortment of minerals in small, but useful, amounts.

HOW TO PREPARE

To peel easily, press the clove under the flat side of a knife. You can either chop the garlic very finely and crush it with the side of a knife or put it in a garlic crusher.

WAYS TO EAT THIS VEGETABLE

You can eat garlic raw or cooked. Using raw garlic produces a strong, pungent flavour whilst cooking produces a more mellow flavour. The longer you cook it the milder and sweeter the flavour. It is usually used in small amounts, say two or three cloves to a dish, but some traditional recipes suggest up to 30 or 40. Garlic burns easily, so take care when you fry or sauté it. Garlic can be added to lots of dishes – vegetable dishes, meats, soups, dips, stir-fries and casseroles. Try rubbing a clove around a salad bowl to give your salad a special taste or tossing 8–10 whole unpeeled cloves into a roasting pan with meat or vegetables. As a stunningly aromatic side vegetable, cut a whole head in half and roast in a little olive oil. Alternatively you can squeeze the roasted flesh paste out and use for flavouring in a whole range of dishes.

AVAILABLE TO PURCHASE
Available all year round.

Tomato couscous salad

So quick and delicious. Great with any meal – any season!

1 cup couscous

1 cup boiling water

5 tomatoes, chopped

1 cup chopped fresh parsley

¼ cup chopped fresh mint leaves

2 cloves crushed garlic

3 Tbsp lemon juice

1 Tbsp sugar

1 Tbsp light olive oil

freshly ground black pepper

Soak the couscous in the water until the water is completely absorbed, about 5 minutes. Combine all ingredients in a bowl and toss gently. Serves 4–6.

TIPS
FOR HOME
GARDENERS

Suitable to plant: nationwide.

When to plant: mid winter or thereabouts.

Approx time till harvest: 6 months.

Depth to plant: 5cm in warm areas; 10cm in areas with cold winters.

Spacing between rows: 40–50cm.

Spacing between plants: 10–15cm.

Water requirements: a moist well-drained soil produces the best heads of garlic.

Fresh herbs, garnishes & edible flowers

The plants featured in this section are those which are commercially available for culinary purposes.

Angelica

(October–April) The leaves of ornamental angelica pachycarp make a wonderful garnish as the shiny dark leaves stay fresh for a while. Another type of angelica, angelica archangelica, is the culinary and medicinal plant. It has matt green leaves which wilt quickly. The stems are used to crystallise for garnish on cakes and desserts, and the root is used for medicinal purposes.

Bay

(Available all year) Bay leaves are used to flavour stocks, stews, marinades and soups. They are generally added at the beginning of cooking and removed before eating. Fresh leaves have lots more flavour than dried ones. Bay is the basis of much French cooking. Bouquet garni has many variations but a bay leaf is essential.

Chervil

(April–October) Chervil is a mild herb and a generous quantity of chopped leaves is best added fresh just before serving as the light flavour is quickly lost. It can be put in all sorts of salads, or sprinkled over lightly-cooked vegetables or soups. Chervil is much like parsley but is more subtle. It goes well with egg dishes, meats, poultry and fish.

Chives

(All year round with supply most plentiful September–May) Chives are a member of the onion family and have a mild onion flavour. They are a really versatile herb with lots of uses – garnishing, in salads, in vegetable and egg dishes, with fish, chicken and mild flavoured meats. Chives should be added to a dish just before serving because too much heat can destroy the flavour. Garlic chives are also available. The leaves of garlic chives are flat, not hollow and circular as in standard chives, and they have the distinctive taste of garlic.

Basil

(Fully available November to April, more limited supplies for rest of year) Many varieties of basil with differing leaves and intensity of flavour are available. These include sweet basil, the most commonly found; dark opal, a dark purple leafed basil; lettuce leaf basil, which has very large green leaves; and fino verde, which is green with very small leaves.

Basil has a sweet strong spicy flavour which will improve almost all salads and savoury dishes. It goes particularly well with tomatoes and is the key ingredient of pesto sauce, along with olive oil, garlic, pine nuts and parmesan cheese. Basil is best used either raw or added at the end of cooking. Basil has many medicinal uses and is also known to deter flies.

Borage

(October–April) Borage tastes refreshing and cooling with a slightly bitter cucumber flavour. The light purple flowers are most commonly used and look great as a garnish on salads or desserts. The leaves are not really that palatable as they are 'hairy' or slightly 'prickly'. If you do use them for their taste select the small young leaves. They can be used raw in salads or lightly cooked with other green vegetables. The flowers can be set in ice cubes or crystallised, both of which look very impressive.

Calendula flowers

(Available all year) The petals of calendulas can be plucked and added to salads for added colour. They are mainly used for decoration as there is little flavour.

Coriander (cilantro)

(All year round) Fresh coriander has a distinctive strong aromatic and spicy flavour. Coriander leaves, stems, roots and seeds are used. The seeds may be used whole or ground and are one of the main ingredients of curry powder, hence coriander is found in many Indian recipes. Fresh coriander leaves are often added to chutneys, salads, stir-fries, curries and sauces. They are used a lot in Chinese, Thai and Indian recipes.

Cornflowers

(November–May) The petals of cornflowers can be plucked and added to salads for a colourful salad. Blue cornflowers are more likely to be found though the pink and whites are also edible.

Curly kale

(All year round) The intense colouring of the leaves makes curly kale a particularly stunning garnish. This is especially true in winter when other garnishes may be difficult to obtain. Some varieties of green kale are also known as collards or winter greens. These can be cooked as a side vegetable in a similar manner to other cabbage types. It is necessary to remove the thick stalks before cooking.

Dill

(October–April) Dill leaves and seeds have a mild aniseed flavour which is similar to though slightly sweeter and more aromatic than, fennel. Small quantities of freshly chopped dill taste great in fish dishes and pickles, with steamed vegetables, salads, soups, egg dishes and sauces. If fresh dill is not available, fennel can be used as a substitute.

Fennel

(October –April) Fennel grows wild by the roadside and may even be in your garden! It looks a bit like dill and tastes much the same. Small quantities of the leaves can be chopped up finely and put in salads or sprinkled over steamed vegetables. Fennel goes well with fish, soups, egg dishes and sauces. The seeds are used too, and have a stronger flavour. Bronze fennel has distinctive dark feathery leaves and makes a particularly stunning garnish. It tastes similar to green fennel. Fennel bulb is also available. It can be sliced finely and added to stir-fries or salads. It also may be baked.

Horseradish

(Roots: April–May, Leaves: October–May) Horseradish is a hot tasting root which is scrubbed, peeled and grated. Small amounts of grated horseradish may be added to salads or steamed vegetables as a flavouring. It can also be mixed with lemon juice, vinegar and/or cream or sour cream to make horseradish cream or sauce – a perfect accompaniment to beef, smoked fish and egg dishes. Horseradish loses much of its piquancy when added to hot dishes. Young leaves are excellent in salads and sandwiches, especially with smoked fish.

Lemon balm

(October–April) Lemon balm leaves give a delicate lemon sweet flavour to vegetable and fruit salads, punches, soups, sauces and stuffings. They can be used in place of grated lemon rind.

Lemon grass

(November–April) A common ingredient in South East Asian cookery, both the bulbous base and the long lemon-flavoured leaves are used. The base should be peeled and chopped finely before use. It freezes well. Use anywhere you want an aromatic lemony flavour. It is especially nice with fish, chicken, rice and vegetable dishes. Try adding some leaves to water as you cook rice, or wrapping around a whole fish before cooking.

Lovage

(November–April) Lovage leaves have a slightly yeasty flavour and are a welcome addition to salads, casseroles, soups and sauces. Young lovage leaves and stalks can be chopped and simmered or sautéed and used as a vegetable by themselves. Treat as you would celery. Lovage is not very widely available.

Marigold

(November–April) Marigold flowers, very similar to calendula, make an attractive edible garnish for all sorts of dishes. They can also be added sparingly to salads. The petals can be used in place of saffron and will give colour in many dishes, especially rice and egg dishes.

Marjoram

See Oregano.

Mint

(Available all year) Mint, one of the most popular herbs in New Zealand, is exceptionally good for flavouring salads, dressings, sauces and soups. Finely chopped mint sprinkled over salads and lightly-cooked spring vegetables is always popular. Whole leaves are an attractive garnish in desserts, fruit juice or punch. There are many varieties of mint available, including apple mint, pineapple mint, peppermint and spearmint. Apple mint is available commercially and has soft textured leaves which are slightly rounded and variegated with cream.

Vietnamese mint

(Vietnamese coriander)

(October – April) This has pointed leaves which are darker than standard mint. They are sometimes lightly variegated with a dull dark red. Vietnamese mint has a strong flavour, and as the name suggests, is used a lot in Asian cooking.

Nasturtium

(September–April) The leaves and flowers can be eaten in salads. Choose young leaves which have a refreshing peppery taste not unlike watercress. Nasturtium seeds when pickled are used as a substitute for capers. Nasturtium is generally not grown commercially in New Zealand as the flowers are so delicate that they damage very easily.

Oregano

(October–April) Oregano tastes really good in omelettes, stuffings, pizzas, salad dressings, mayonnaise, pasta, sausage, rice dishes and most vegetable dishes, particularly tomatoes, egg plant, courgettes and potatoes. It can be used to flavour vinegars. There are many varieties which have been developed from a parent plant, oregano or wild marjoram. In New Zealand we tend to use the names oregano, marjoram or sweet marjoram interchangeably and although they are different varieties they are very similar. Oregano is much more widely available.

Parsley

(All year) Parsley is probably the most commonly used herb in New Zealand. It is extremely versatile and can be used with a wide range of foods including most salads, vegetables, soups, stews, dressings, meat and fish dishes. If adding to a cooked dish, it is better to add parsley at the end of cooking because flavour is lost with prolonged heating. Italian parsley is also available. Whilst having a similar taste to standard parsley, the leaves are flat, not curly, and they look a little bit like coriander.

Pansy

(All year) Hearts Ease pansy is an attractive edible flower which is used for garnish. It is available commercially in limited quantities.

Rosemary

(All year) Rosemary is a strong-flavoured herb which is generally used in small amounts. It goes well with lamb, mutton and beef. Rosemary is often used in stuffings and marinades. Vegetables like kumara, parsnip, garlic, onion or potatoes, are fantastic when roasted with olive oil and fresh rosemary leaves. Add at the beginning of cooking so the full aromatic flavour can permeate the food. Whole leaves and the attractive light purple flowers are often used as a garnish. Rosemary sprigs also make excellent flavoured oils and vinegars.

Sage

(October–April) Sage is a strong-flavoured herb which is generally used in small quantities. It is quite a versatile herb which lends itself well to a range of dishes including rich meats, stuffings, onions, soups, sauces, dressings, patés, quiches, pulses, cheese dishes, breads and casseroles. There are several varieties of sage, some of which do not have the green leaves of standard sage. Pineapple sage is available commercially and is generally sweeter and more mellow. Try threading whole leaves onto skewers with cubes of meat and vegetables.

Salad burnet

(October–April) Salad burnet has a very delicate and pleasant flavour. It is sometimes described as being like a cucumber with a slightly almond taste. It should always be used raw as it tastes bitter when cooked. As the name suggests salad burnet is great in salads. Use only the very young leaves and discard the stems. It is also a very attractive garnish.

Tarragon

(November–April) French tarragon is the most commonly found variety. Raw or cooked tarragon goes well with most vegetable dishes, especially those with a delicate flavour. It is used with chicken, fish, mild meat and egg dishes, in salads, sauces, dressings and makes a lovely flavoured vinegar. Tarragon is a key ingredient of bearnaise sauce.

Savory

(October–April) There are two types of savory, summer savory and winter savory. Both are available commercially in limited quantities. Both taste a bit like thyme but are hotter and peppery. They can be used raw or cooked, whenever you want a warm-hot flavour. Summer savory has a more delicate flavour than winter savory. Savory can be added to stuffing, sausages, cheese dishes, steamed vegetables and salads.

Thyme

(September–May) There are many varieties of thyme and each has a slightly different flavour. Lemon and standard thyme are available commercially and may be used raw or cooked. Thyme can be added to soups, casseroles, stuffing, chicken, meat, steamed vegetables, salads and dressings, or sprinkled on breads and pizzas. Fresh thyme sprigs steeped in vinegar or oil impart an excellent flavour to marinades, dressings etc. Lemon thyme has a more subtle flavour. Pizza thyme, as the name suggests, is great on pizzas.

Sorrel

(Seldom available commercially) Sorrel has a sharp taste and gives soups, sauces, omelettes and salads a tangy and refreshing flavour. Sorrel goes well with spinach and silver beet dishes or indeed can replace spinach in a recipe. It has an attractive leaf which looks a bit like young spinach and is a good addition to a green mixed leaf salad.

Verbena

(December–April) Lemon verbena is available commercially and can be used raw to impart a subtle lemon flavour to salads or drinks. Verbena flowers are great garnishes and are available in white and a range of pinks/reds.

WHAT TO LOOK FOR
Choose clean, crisp leaves or flowers.

HOW TO KEEP
Refrigerate in their original packaging or plastic bags in the crisper. Make sure leaves aren't squashed. Alternatively, if the herbs are still growing with the roots attached, place the roots in a jar of water and do not refrigerate.

NUTRITIONAL VALUE
For most people herbs are eaten in small quantities so they are more important for their great taste than nutritional value. Many herbs are reputed to have different health enhancing properties.

HOW TO PREPARE
Remove any coarse or wilted leaves. Soaking the leaves in warm water for 3–4 minutes followed by refrigeration for 15–20 minutes can refresh the leaves if necessary.

AVAILABLE TO PURCHASE
Most fresh herbs are available all year round although supply tends to be more limited in winter months. See individual listings for a more precise guide. Hydroponic growing has extended the season ensuring a more reliable supply.

TIPS
FOR HOME
GARDENERS

Salad or annual herbs tend to be seasonal, and include basil, chillies, chives, coriander, and dill. Perennial herbs such as tarragon, horseradish and to a lesser extent chives disappear at the end of the growing season and appear the following year. Cooking herbs are generally perennials and are available all year round. They include bay, garlic, marjoram, mint, oregano, parsley, rosemary, sage and thyme. Most have a stronger flavour than the salad herbs.

Most herbs and edible flowers are easy to grow in a moderately fertile soil that is both moist and well drained. Some, such as basil, require a daily watering if they are to flourish.

Indian vegetables

As the population of Indian people living in New Zealand gets larger there is an increasing range of Indian vegetables becoming available. Some of these vegetables are more readily available than others.

A Indian marrow
(Lauki or white gourd)

This is a light green marrow which can grow up to a metre long. The marrow is peeled and the skins removed. It is often rolled into balls or diced and cooked with split peas or dhals in a curry.

B Ribbed gourd (Turia)

Peel and cut into chunks to use typically in a curry. Seeds may or may not be removed.

C Bitter melon
(Karela, fu quas)

As the name implies these really are bitter! To use, cut in half or remove the end or ends, scoop out the seeds. Do not peel. To remove some of the bitterness, they are sometimes blanched in boiling water or salted for 15 minutes and rinsed prior to cooking. They are generally either stuffed with a vegetable or meat filling or sliced finely and stir-fried with curry until dry and crisp. These are also used in Chinese cooking where one of the traditional Cantonese dishes is to stir-fry sliced bitter melon with beef and serve it in black bean sauce.

D Snake beans

These are also used in Indian cookery. See beans.

E Indian beans (Papadi)

There are lots of different varieties of beans grown. Most are shelled and used either on their own or in a curry with vegetables, such as onion, tomato, and egg plant. Some varieties are more tender and smaller. With these the whole pod is used – similar to using snow peas. Generally these small papadi are curried, often with potato or kumara.

F Tindori (Tindora)

This looks a lot like a gherkin. It is generally sliced lengthwise and added to curries. Cook slowly until tender. It cannot be eaten raw.

G Curry leaves

Used for flavouring in all Indian cookery. The leaves are used whole and can be dried like a bay leaf.

H Taro leaves

The tender leaves of taro are used in Indian cookery. A paste is made of pea flour, chilli, garlic, lemon juice, garam marsala and water. This paste is spread over the washed and dried leaves which are then folded into small packages. Older leaves need to be steamed first. The packages are then slowly cooked in a little oil. Once tender they are sprinkled with coconut, green coriander and sugar and served hot or cold.

Cow peas (Chori)

These are about 12–15cm in length and are used for beans only, not the pod. There are several varieties available and colour varies from red, white to green. They are used in soups, stir-fries and curries. When dried they are known as the black eye bean.

Pigeon peas (Toover)

These look similar to standard green peas, although the colour of the pod may vary from light to dark green depending on the variety. They are commonly podded, just like peas, and used to make a curry with potatoes. They are also used like papadi. When dried, pigeon peas are used to make dahl.

WHAT TO LOOK FOR

Look for product that appears crisp and fresh, showing no signs of deterioration.

HOW TO KEEP

Store in a cool place or in the warmest part of your refrigerator.

NUTRITIONAL VALUE

The beans and peas supply a good source of fibre, some vitamins and protein.

AVAILABLE TO PURCHASE

Most Indian vegetables are available from December until March in limited quantities. Imported supplies supplement New Zealand grown produce when out of season here.

TIPS
FOR HOME
GARDENERS

Most of these require a warm fertile, frost-free garden. Regular supplies of water are also important in order to grow most Indian vegetables.

Curried vegetables

Delicious one-dish no-fuss cooking at its best!

5–10 snake beans, cut in quarters

10–12 small waxy potatoes, cut in quarters

1 cup Indian marrow, diced

1 onion, peeled and cut into wedges

1–2 Tbsp mild curry paste

165g can coconut milk

Place all ingredients in a baking dish and mix well. Cover and bake at 180°C for 40 minutes or until the potatoes are tender. Serve with poppadums and garnish with fresh coriander. Serves 4.

Kohlrabi

Translated from German, kohlrabi means cabbage-turnip. Kohlrabi is milder and sweeter than both cabbage and turnip. Whilst looking like a root vegetable, it is a stem vegetable which swells to a turnip shape above the ground. It is a member of the Brassica family.

WHAT TO LOOK FOR

Select kohlrabi about the size of a tennis ball or smaller. Look for thin, tender and unblemished skin. Avoid soft or wrinkled produce.

HOW TO KEEP

Refrigerate in plastic bags.

NUTRITIONAL VALUE

It is a brassica and contains a range of phytochemicals. It provides an excellent source of vitamin C, and a good source of folate.

HOW TO PREPARE

It should be prepared similarly to turnips. Cut off the base and trim the stalks. Cook before peeling to retain maximum flavour. Boil, steam or microwave whole if they are small, otherwise slice first.

WAYS TO EAT THIS VEGETABLE

Kohlrabi is served mainly as a side vegetable, steamed, mashed or in a stir-fry. It may also be baked, added to casseroles and soups. It can be used raw in salads.

AVAILABLE TO PURCHASE

Limited quantities in winter months.

TIPS FOR HOME GARDENERS

Suitable to plant: nationwide.

When to plant: summer, autumn and spring.

Approx time till harvest: 6–8 weeks.

Depth to plant: 5cm.

Spacing between rows: 30cm.

Spacing between plants: 20cm.

Roasted kohlrabi and winter vegetables

2 Tbsp olive oil

2 kohlrabi, ends and knobs trimmed, and cut into chunks

1 parsnip, ends trimmed, peeled, and cut into chunks

2 carrots, ends trimmed, peeled and cut into chunks

2 Tbsp olive oil

1–2 garlic cloves, crushed

sea salt to taste

Place all ingredients in a roasting pan. Toss with oil and garlic to coat. Bake at 200°C for 25–35 minutes or until golden brown and tender. Turn over several times during cooking. Garnish if desired and salt. Serves 4.

Kumara

Kumara is also known as the sweet potato. It has been grown and eaten in New Zealand since the Maori first came to New Zealand, brought by Kupe in about the 10th century from Hawaiki. This variety was a bush with tubers much smaller than the kumara we know today. Later the bigger sweet potato was introduced, which came to be known as the kumara too. It grows on a creeping vine and is the one we eat now. The majority of our kumara is grown in Northland in the Northern Wairoa region where soil type and climatic conditions suit kumara perfectly.

There are a huge number of different varieties of kumara, although only three are commercially available in New Zealand. The most common is red-skinned, Owairaka Red, with a creamy white flesh sold as Red. Gold kumara, sometimes sold as Toka Toka Gold, has a golden skin and flesh and has a sweeter taste than red. Orange kumara, sometimes sold as Beauregard, has a rich orange flesh and is sweeter than both red and gold.

WHAT TO LOOK FOR
Look for kumara which is firm with smooth and unbroken skin. Date stamped product gives a reliable measure of freshness. Buy regularly, no more than a week's supply.

HOW TO KEEP
Like potatoes, kumara should be stored in a cool, dark place which is well ventilated. Do not refrigerate.

NUTRITIONAL VALUE
Kumara is a valuable source of vitamin C, iron, potassium and calcium. The coloured skin and flesh of kumara carries an array of phytochemicals. Varieties with red or purple skins or flesh contain anthocyanins, and those with orange and yellow pigments are rich in β-carotene. The richer the colour the more anthocyanins and β-carotene present.

HOW TO PREPARE
Kumara can be prepared in exactly the same way as potatoes. It's not always necessary to peel them. If possible, scrub thoroughly and leave the skin on.

WAYS TO EAT THIS VEGETABLE
Boiled, mashed, roasted, in soups, stir-fries, on barbecues, or in pies or quiches, kumara is a very versatile vegetable. Traditionally they were cooked in a hangi. They can be baked or stuffed as you would potatoes. Chunks of kumara are great in casseroles. Roasting unpeeled kumara in long thin strips with peppers and onions drizzled in oil and balsamic vinegar and flavoured with honey, ginger and garlic is amazing! Grated or finely sliced kumara is good added to a stuffing. Kumara chips are tasty, prepared and served as you would potato wedges, or slice thinly and they puff up into delicious crisps. Kumara salads are wonderful. Cook the kumara first, either microwave, boil or steam until softened. You can peel but it is not necessary. Try using a combination of the three varieties in salads or when roasting – this looks and tastes great. Kumara goes particularly well with sweetish meats such as chicken and pork. They also complement fruits such as banana, pineapple, apricot and apple well.

AVAILABLE TO PURCHASE
Kumara are available all year round.

Suitable to plant: frost free areas nationwide.

When to plant: mid to late spring.

Approx time till harvest: 8–12 weeks.

Depth to plant: plant shoots 10cm deep. Plant tubers 15cm deep.

Spacing between rows: 50cm.

Spacing between plants: 50cm.

Water requirements: plant in moist yet well-drained soil.

Char roasted mix

The intense flavour of roasted vegetables is really enhanced by the wonderful garlic and lemon tastes in this recipe. Try it – you'll be hooked!

2 medium kumara, sliced lengthwise

2 onions, cut into wedges

2 medium peppers, deseeded and sliced

3 courgettes or 1 medium egg plant, sliced

2 cloves garlic, crushed

¼ cup olive oil

¼ cup lemon juice

2 Tbsp brown sugar

freshly ground black pepper

Place the prepared vegetables in a baking dish. When cutting the onions, leave part of the base on so the wedge stays together when cooked. Combine the garlic, oil, lemon juice, sugar and pepper. Pour over the vegetables. Mix to coat evenly. Bake at 200°C for 25–35 minutes or until tender and golden brown. Alternatively cook on a medium to hot barbecue plate for about 10–15 minutes or until tender. Serves 4.

Leeks

Leeks have been the national emblem of Wales since 640 AD when, according to legend, the Welsh defeated the invading Saxons because they had leeks attached to their hats. The leeks prevented them from attacking each other by mistake!

Leeks belong to the onion family and look a bit like a huge spring onion, with a mild onion flavour. Miniature leeks are sometimes available.

WHAT TO LOOK FOR
Choose well-shaped, medium stems with fresh green tops and lots of white flesh.

HOW TO KEEP
Refrigerate in plastic bags.

NUTRITIONAL VALUE
Leeks contain excellent amounts of vitamin C as well as folate and useful amounts of B vitamins, vitamin E, copper, potassium and iron. A range of saponins are present with some flavonoids. Carotenoids and chlorophyll are contained mainly in the green tops.

HOW TO PREPARE
Trim the root end and trim off the green tops – leaving about 10cm of green. Remove any outer leaves which are coarse or damaged. Make a slit down the length of the green stem and rinse thoroughly in cold running water. Sometimes dirt gets trapped – this is because leeks are 'earthed up' to keep them white.

TIPS
FOR HOME
GARDENERS

Suitable to plant: nationwide.

When to plant: spring, summer and autumn.

Approx time till harvest: 8 weeks.

Depth to plant: plant strong seedlings 10–15cm deep.

Spacing between rows: 15cm.

Spacing between plants. 10–15cm.

Water requirements: leeks resent dry conditions.

WAYS TO EAT THIS VEGETABLE

Leeks can be used as a side vegetable - microwaved, boiled, steamed or stir-fried. Traditionally they are served with a white or cheese sauce. Ham or bacon teams particularly well with leeks. They are also excellent in soups, flans, pies and casseroles. Cooked cold leeks can make interesting salads. A small amount of finely sliced raw leek, white ends only, makes a tasty addition to salads by adding a mild onion-type taste. You can also use leek as a wrap as you would filo pastry; just slit down one side of the leek and peel into sheets. Use this to wrap up fillings.

AVAILABLE TO PURCHASE

Although they are thought of as a winter vegetable, leeks are usually available all year round. Sometimes they are hard to get between November and February.

Leek and potato soup

This delicious soup is just perfect for those colder nights – quick and easy to make with a flavour that is divine!

2 leeks, sliced

3 potatoes, peeled and chopped

2 Tbsp olive oil

4 cups chicken stock

2 cups milk

Sauté the leek and potato in the oil until softened. Add the stock and simmer gently for 15–20 minutes or until the vegetables are tender. Purée if wished. Add the milk. Heat but do not boil.

Lettuces

Originally grown in the Mediterranean region, lettuce has always been a popular vegetable. The Greeks and Romans not only ate lettuces, but used them medicinally to induce sleep.

There are now many lettuce varieties, with available varieties changing often. From totally green to multi-coloured, leafy and crisp to dense and firm, mild and subtle to piquant and intense – there are literally hundreds of brilliant combinations of taste, variety, texture and nutrition! The situation is made even more confusing when seed companies market similar products with different names. The term 'lettuce' includes a host of different cultivars (varieties) and even non-lettuces such as endive.

Lettuces can be divided into:

Head lettuces: Iceberg types are the most popular and are sometimes called normal, crisphead or standard lettuce.

Leafy lettuces: These are loose leaf lettuces and have no heart.

Other greens: e.g. endive, frisee and a host of salad greens.

Iceberg

This is sometimes called normal, crisphead or standard lettuce. The heads are firm and tightly packed with a central core or heart. The leaves are crunchy and have a mild flavour. The outer leaves are a darker green than the central pale leaves. Cupped leaves hold their shape and are often used to hold fillings. Frillice is a similar lettuce variety which is gaining in popularity. It is characterised by its deep green colour and leaves which are very frilled at the edges.

Cosberg

A cross between iceberg and a cos lettuce, it has boat shaped leaves and the taste of an iceberg with a hint of Christmas green peas. Its crunchy texture is suited to salads.

Butterhead or buttercrunch

This is a green lettuce with loose leaves. It has a soft texture and flat smooth succulent leaves which have a delicate buttery feel and flavour. Some varieties have heart-shaped leaves while others are more rounded. Red buttercrunch or red butterhead are also available.

Red oak, red salad bowl, red sails, green oak and green salad bowl

These are loose leaf lettuces and have no heart. They have a green-red or red leaf which can be soft. They are sweet-tasting.

Green coral, green frill, lollo bionda, red coral, red frill and lollo rossa

These are very similar lettuces. All have attractive crinkly leaves that stand up on a plate. They have a sharp and slightly bitter flavour. The depth of red or green colour depends on the variety and the season.

Cos

This is an old-fashioned winter lettuce which is also known as Romaine. It has an elongated head with coarse leaves that are crunchy and sharp in flavour. This is a key ingredient of Caesar salad.

Endive

The endive is often classed as a lettuce but is actually from the celery family. There are two main types, curly endive and fine leaf. They have a slightly bitter flavour.

WHAT TO LOOK FOR
Choose lettuces with clean, crisp leaves.

HOW TO KEEP
Refrigerate in plastic bags or in the crisper. Make sure the lettuce isn't squashed. Alternatively, if the lettuce still has roots attached, place the roots in a jar of water and do not refrigerate.

NUTRITIONAL VALUE
The common belief that lettuce is a 'nutritional desert' does not do this vegetable justice, particularly the newer cultivars. Most lettuces have a range of nutrients, including vitamin C, vitamin E, folate, iron, fibre and β-carotene. New cultivars are more often strongly coloured than the traditional varieties, and the pigments that give them the colour have a range of nutritional benefits. Most cultivars contain the pigments β-carotene, lutein, zeaxanthin and chlorophyll. The red cultivars additionally contain anthocyanins. Whilst it is true that lettuce is composed largely of water, this is an advantage in giving low calorie 'bulk', which is important in terms of satiety or keeping you feeling 'full'. Because lettuce is eaten so often the nutritional contribution can be quite high.

HOW TO PREPARE
Remove any coarse or wilted leaves. You can use these in soups. Gently tear lettuce leaves. If you cut the leaves, the lettuce won't look as good and you'll damage the cells, releasing an enzyme that will destroy the vitamin C. If necessary, soaking the leaves in warm water for 3–4 minutes followed by refrigeration can refresh the leaves making them crisper. Dry the lettuce well after washing; a salad spinner is really helpful.

WAYS TO EAT THIS VEGETABLE
Lettuce is mostly used raw in salads. You can make all sorts of wonderful salads and garnishes with the different lettuces. Using several varieties together increases interest. Lettuce leaves may also be used as wraps.

AVAILABLE TO PURCHASE
With the new varieties and the use of hydroponics and greenhouses, lettuces are now available all year round.

Potatoes and blue cheese salad

Succulent roasted vegetables tossed between crisp leaves and drizzled with your favourite vinaigrette have all the elements of an exceptionally good salad! The potatoes and blue cheese are a particularly yummy combination.

12 small baby gourmet potatoes, halved

olive oil for spraying

¼ cup walnut halves

100g creamy blue cheese, sliced

1 avocado, cut into wedges

5 handfuls red leafed lettuce

2–3 Tbsp vinaigrette e.g. balsamic

Place the potatoes on an oven tray. Spray with olive oil. Bake at 200°C for 20–25 minutes. Add the walnuts, bake another 5 minutes. Allow to cool slightly on a serving platter and add the rest of the ingredients. Toss the vinaigrette through the salad. Serves 4.

TIPS
FOR HOME GARDENERS

Suitable to plant: nationwide depending on the variety chosen.

When to plant: year round.

Approx time till harvest: 4–6 weeks.

Depth to plant: 5cm.

Spacing between rows: 30cm depending on the variety chosen.

Spacing between plants: 20–30cm depending on the variety.

Water requirements: regular supplies of water are essential for the development of crisp succulent lettuce.

Urenika

Māori potatoes taewa (riwai)

Before the primary European settlement of Aotearoa, around 1840, the taewa (riwai) was a staple food crop of the Māori. Taewa is a collective noun referring to the 'Māori' potato, a collection of varieties of Solanum tuberosum now cultivated by Māori for at least 200 years. Māori acknowledge that some varieties arrived with early explorers such as Captain James Cook and the French explorer, Marion du Fresne, along with sealers and whalers during the eighteenth century. Māori were quick to recognise the advantages these new introductions had over other traditional food sources.

There are many varieties of Māori potato; these include Tutaekuri (also known as Urenika), Makoikoi, Moe Moe, Raupi, Te Māori, Karuparera and Huakaroro – all have quite differing appearances.

Karuparera

WHAT TO LOOK FOR

Choose even-sized potatoes which are free of blemishes. Their unusual appearance sets them apart from standard potatoes. Differing varieties vary markedly in size, skin and flesh colour. Skin colour and size is also dependent on growing conditions, soil type and the weather. They usually have a purple/black skin, with deep-set eyes that are either purple or white. The flesh is waxy and coloured rich yellow, white, or purple. Like standard potatoes, flesh type ranges from waxy to floury-textured, however most varieties tend to be waxy.

HOW TO KEEP

Māori potatoes do not need refrigeration, and are best stored in a cool, dark, dry place. They are best eaten within ten days of harvest.

NUTRITIONAL VALUE

Like potatoes, Māori potatoes are an excellent source of vitamin C and fibre. They also contain some potassium, thiamine, folate and magnesium. They are high in starch so they will stop you feeling hungry for a long time. Yellow flesh and/or red skinned potatoes are nutritionally preferable because of their higher antioxidant levels.

HOW TO PREPARE

They boil and steam particularly well and taste reminiscent of new potatoes with a sweet flavour and a smooth texture. The skin is very tender and peeling is both unnecessary and, because of their irregular shape, difficult.

WAYS TO EAT THIS VEGETABLE

Māori potatoes tend to be incorporated into meals as we would other potatoes. Traditionally cooked in a hangi, they suit moist baking conditions and are especially good steamed.

AVAILABLE TO PURCHASE

Māori potatoes are available in limited quantities with better supply in the summer months.

Suitable to plant: nationwide depending on the variety and season.

When to plant: late winter and spring in frost free areas. Elsewhere spring and summer.

Approx time till harvest: 8–10 weeks depending on variety.

Depth to plant: 10cm.

Spacing between rows: 40–50cm.

Spacing between plants: 40cm.

Water requirements: supply with regular moisture in dry weather.

Māori potatoes with warm dressing

The mix of different coloured potatoes sure makes this look cool! This is a dish that tastes great hot, warm or chilled and may be served on a bed of watercress, spinach or lettuce leaves as a salad, or as a side dish.

1 medium red onion, diced
¼ cup olive oil
¼ cup lemon juice or 3 Tbsp good quality vinegar
2 Tbsp honey
freshly ground black pepper
4–5 Māori potatoes (400g), washed and sliced into bite-sized chunks
3–4 salad or boiling (waxy) potatoes (400g), cut into bite-sized chunks

Combine the diced red onion, oil, lemon juice, honey and pepper. Set aside while you cook the potatoes. Place the prepared potatoes in a saucepan. Cover with cold water. Bring to the boil and simmer, uncovered for 7–10 minutes or until the potatoes are just tender. (The cooking water will go an amazing purple colour, but don't worry, it won't affect the colour of the potatoes!) Drain the cooking water from the potatoes and while they are still warm, pour over the dressing, shaking the pot or gently stirring to coat evenly. Allow to sit for a few minutes before serving to let the flavours mingle. You may add herbs like mint or coriander to the dressing or as a garnish. Serves 4.

Watermelon

Honeydew

Prince melon

Rock melon

Melons

Melons are of Asian origin and were first transplanted to Italy and then to France, well before the 16th century. Melons are related to the family of summer squash which includes marrows and courgettes.

There are hundreds of varieties of melons and the four most popular in New Zealand are watermelon, rock melon, honey dew and prince melon. Of these four, only the rock melon has orange coloured pigments. Orange fleshed melons contain some of the same key components and deliver similar health benefits as other yellow/orange vegetables.

Watermelon

Most commonly watermelons are large with green skin and pale green stripes. The flesh is dark pink and very juicy with characteristic black flat glossy seeds. Seedless varieties are available. Yellow flesh varieties are also sometimes available. Skin colour varies with variety and pale green skins are also found.

Netted melon

Similar to a rock melon although the netting is finer and the flesh is a pale green. It has a mild, sweet flavour. Green and red netted varieties are available.

Rock melon (cantaloupe)

A soft peach-coloured flesh which has a distinctive aroma and sweet smooth musky flavour. Rock melons are smaller than watermelons and have a coarsely netted skin.

Honeydew (white melon)

This melon is slightly elongated and has greenish/white skin with a pale green/cream flesh.

Prince melon (Derishi)

This melon has a cream/green skin and green or orange-coloured flesh. It has a sweet full flavour.

TIPS
FOR HOME
GARDENERS

Suitable to plant: frost free areas.

When to plant: spring and summer.

Approx time till harvest: 10–12 weeks.

Depth to plant: 5cm.

Spacing between rows: 30–40cm.

Spacing between plants: 30–40cm.

Water requirements: supply with regular quantities of moisture particularly during dry weather.

WHAT TO LOOK FOR

Watermelon: A strong contrast of dark and light stripes is a good indication of ripeness.

Rockmelon and green netted: These melons have a porous skin and the exotic aroma is the best indication of ripeness. The melons should be firm with no signs of soft spots or mould on the skin as this indicates over-ripeness.

Honeydew and prince: When ripe these melons will yield gently to pressure at the flower end, not the stem end. Avoid those which are soft, bruised or damaged.

HOW TO KEEP

Ripen at room temperature and store in the refrigerator. Cut surfaces should be covered with a plastic film. Use promptly. Rock melons stored in the fridge may taint other ingredients such as butter, milk and cheese, so keep storage time as short as possible.

NUTRITIONAL VALUE

Despite their high water content, melons have high levels of vitamin C and moderate levels of potassium. Rock melons, with their orange flesh, contain β-carotene which is converted to vitamin A in the body. Watermelon, with its red flesh, contains a different carotenoid, lycopene. Rock melon, honeydew and watermelon contain some phenolic compounds, and all melons are very low in calories.

HOW TO PREPARE

Remove seeds and skin prior to eating. Watermelons are often available seedless or with very small seeds which are edible.

WAYS TO EAT THIS VEGETABLE

All melons are delicious chilled and eaten as a fruit dessert or an ideal snack. They are great in salads, both sweet and savoury, used as the base for drinks and are wonderful garnishes.

AVAILABLE TO PURCHASE

Depending on the variety chosen, New Zealand grown melons are available in the summer months from December until April. Imported varieties ensure almost year round supply.

Bean and melon salad

Simple and stunning, this green salad is really refreshing and has a delicious combination of flavours.

20–25 green beans, trimmed

12–15 snow peas, trimmed

¼ prince melon, peeled and cut into chunks

1 Tbsp lemon juice

1 Tbsp sugar

1 Tbsp oil

Blanch the beans and snow peas in boiling water for 2–3 minutes. Cool under cold running water. Drain. Mix the prince melon, beans and snow peas together. Blend the lemon juice, sugar and oil together. Pour over the salad. Mix well. Serves 4.

Microgreens

Recently entering the New Zealand market, microgreens are simply seedlings of herbs and salad greens we already know. They offer many exciting new textures, colours and flavours. Being such immature plants the flavour is exceptionally intense. They have a strikingly fresh miniature appearance and this presents a whole new range of cuisine options. This has been realised in the food service industry, where microgreens are growing quickly in popularity. They are a particularly popular addition to salads and make stunning edible garnishes.

Microgreens can be grown from the seed of almost any vegetable. They are harvested at 7–21 days after planting and are sold as blends (Asian, French etc.) of different seeds as well as single varieties like coriander, rocket, red chard, basil, sango and watercress.

Asian blend

Combi

Watercress

Sango

Rocket

Coriander

Italian parsley

Red chard

WHAT TO LOOK FOR
Crisp leaves with vibrant colouring.

HOW TO KEEP
Refrigerate in plastic bags or in the crisper. Use within 5 to 6 days of purchase.

NUTRITIONAL VALUE
As microgreens are seedlings of vegetables and herbs their nutritional profile is probably similar to the mature plant although levels will vary.

WAYS TO EAT
Use as a garnish for a dish of complementary flavour to the microgreen. Try microgreens for giving an interesting accent to anything you like - from soups to sauces to meat dishes to desserts.

AVAILABLE TO PURCHASE
Supply of microgreens is limited. A range of varieties ensures all year round supply.

TIPS
FOR HOME
GARDENERS

Suitable to plant: nationwide. Many can also be raised indoors.

When to plant: all year.

Approx time till harvest: 2 weeks depending on warmth.

Depth to plant: shallowly.

Water requirements: constant moisture is essential for the raising of microgreens.

Potato and chicken salad with rocket

600g new or salad potatoes, scrubbed and halved

10–12 cherry tomatoes, halved or 6 small tomatoes, quartered

½ telegraph cucumber, diced

3 cups rocket leaves

1 Tbsp vegetable oil

3 boneless chicken breasts, skinned and cut into strips

2 Tbsp red wine vinegar

1 Tbsp honey

2 Tbsp vegetable oil

Place new potatoes in a pan and cover with water. Simmer for 12–15 minutes or until tender then drain and allow to cool. Mix with tomatoes, cucumber and rocket. Meanwhile heat the first measure of oil in a large frying pan. Add the chicken and stir-fry for 8–10 minutes or until cooked through and browned. Remove from heat. Toss into the salad. In the frying pan, heat vinegar, honey, oil and bring to the boil scraping to remove pan juices. Pour over salad and toss well. Serves 4.

Mushrooms

Mushrooms have been eaten in Europe, Russia, China and Japan for thousands of years. Through their history they have been thought to have had certain magical powers or have been used as medicines. There are over 250 edible mushroom varieties throughout the world although only a few are commercially available in New Zealand.

Button mushrooms

These are mushrooms which are harvested when still small and unopened. Once the mushrooms open to a stage where the gills are visible they are generally referred to as cups. White mushrooms are the most commonly consumed mushrooms in New Zealand.

Swiss browns
(brown buttons, gourmet browns)

These have a darker brown top than button or cap mushrooms, but similar looking gills. They are generally harvested when 3–5cm in diameter. Swiss browns have a rich, nutty flavour and are good to use when a stronger flavour is required.

Portabellos (brown flats, flats)

These are Swiss brown mushrooms which have been allowed to grow larger. They are usually harvested when about 8–10cm in diameter, with well formed gills underneath and, of course, flat. They are perfect for stuffing and have a very rich and intense flavour.

Shiitake mushrooms

These have a traditional mushroom shape with a dark brown cap and often with small speckles around the rim. Shiitake mushrooms have a distinctive fresh earthy flavour and aroma and are widely used in Asian cooking. When cooked the shiitake mushrooms retain their shape, have a smooth texture and do not discolour. Shiitake mushrooms are versatile and may be used raw or in all sorts of cooking where flavour infusion takes place.

Oyster or phoenix tail
(abalone, pleurotte)

These very attractive fan shaped mushrooms have a delicate seafood/oyster flavour. The colour can vary from a soft grey to a deep brown. Underneath is a delicate and distinctive fan-shaped gill formation which is a soft cream colour. The shape and flavour make it attractive to serve both raw or lightly cooked in many types of dishes. The flavour is subtle and it does not discolour when cooked.

Swiss browns

Shiitake

Portabellos

Oyster or phoenix tail

TIPS
FOR HOME
GARDENERS

Suitable to plant: nationwide.

When to plant: spring.

Approx time till harvest: 8–12 weeks.

Depth to plant: 8–10cm.

Water requirements: plant in moist well-drained soil.

WHAT TO LOOK FOR

With all mushrooms, the fresher the better. Look for mushrooms with a good colour and avoid any which are damaged, bruised or with signs of deterioration. Where appropriate, gills should be fresh and upright.

HOW TO KEEP

Remove from plastic packaging and refrigerate in a paper bag. Mushrooms continue to grow after harvesting and they will respire or 'sweat' in plastic bags. Brown paper bags will absorb moisture and keep mushrooms fresher.

NUTRITIONAL VALUE

Mushrooms are a moderate source of protein, are high in potassium and low in sodium – which is a desirable balance. They are also a significant source of selenium. Mushrooms are an excellent source of many B group vitamins including folate, niacin, riboflavin, biotin and pantothenic acid. They also supply some fibre and small amounts of other minerals.

HOW TO PREPARE

You don't usually need to peel cultivated mushrooms. Just wipe both the cap and stalk with a paper towel. Field mushrooms sometimes need peeling.

WAYS TO EAT THIS VEGETABLE

Mushrooms are incredibly versatile and will add flavour to many dishes. They can be used with meat, in soups, sauces, on pizzas, in casseroles, in stir-fries, in omelettes, in pies and salads. They can be microwaved, barbecued, stir-fried, baked, grilled, fried or poached. Serve them raw with a dip or in salads.

AVAILABLE TO PURCHASE

All year round. Some minor varieties have limited availability.

Beetroot and mushrooms

The richness of the beetroot, the tangy flavour of horseradish and the mellow taste of the kumara make this combination truly special.

2 medium gold or orange kumara, sliced

2 red onions, peeled and cut into wedges

3 beetroot, unpeeled and cut into wedges

8 whole button mushrooms

2 tsp horseradish sauce

¼ cup olive oil

¼ cup lemon juice

2 Tbsp brown sugar

freshly ground black pepper

Place the prepared vegetables in a baking dish. When cutting the onions, leave part of the base on so the wedge stays together when cooked. Combine the horseradish, oil, lemon juice, sugar and pepper. Pour over the vegetables. Mix to coat evenly. Bake at 200°C for 25–35 minutes or until tender and golden brown. Alternatively cook on a medium to hot barbecue plate for about 10–15 minutes or until tender. Serves 4.

Okra

Okra is thought to have originated in Africa and has spread to become widely used in southern American states, the West Indies, India, Asia and South America. Today okra is an important part of Cajun cooking styles. It is probably best known in New Zealand for being the key ingredient of gumbo which is a stew of okra, tomatoes, chilli and chicken or seafood. Okra is sometimes known as ladies fingers, bhindi and bamia. Okra contains mucilaginous gums which act as a natural thickening agent in soups, curries and casseroles.

There are many varieties of okra; the most commonly found are green and white. Green okra is shorter and slightly stubby when compared with the white okra. White is actually a light green colour and is longer and more slender than green okra, and it has quite pronounced ridges.

WHAT TO LOOK FOR
Good okra must be fresh and small, preferably less than 6–8cm in length. Large okra tends to be tough and stringy.

HOW TO KEEP
Refrigerate in plastic bags. Use promptly. Don't wash before you store them as they will become slimy.

NUTRITIONAL VALUE
Okra is a good source of folate, vitamin C and fibre. They also supply some vitamin B6, iron and riboflavin.

HOW TO PREPARE
The stalk ends are generally removed. Okra can be left whole or sliced. Boil, steam, stir-fry or microwave until soft and tender. Avoid using brass, copper or iron pans as the okra will discolour.

WAYS TO EAT THIS VEGETABLE
Toss freshly cooked okra in lemon juice and a little butter. Okra can be added to curries, soups, casseroles or salads.

AVAILABLE TO PURCHASE
A limited supply is available all year round.

TIPS FOR HOME GARDENERS

Suitable to plant: warm northern parts of the country.

When to plant: November–December. Okra needs very warm soil temperatures to grow. Start seeds indoors at least two months before transplanting.

Approx time till harvest: 50–60 days.

Depth to plant: 5cm.

Spacing between rows: 1 metre.

Spacing between plants: 60x60cm.

Water requirements: every 7–10 days.

Okra with tomatoes

200g okra, washed, trimmed, sliced

1–2 cloves of garlic, peeled and crushed

1 small onion, finely chopped

1 x 410g can whole tomatoes

¼ cup water

salt to taste

Place sliced okra in pan; cover with water. Bring to the boil and cook for 5 minutes. Meanwhile, sauté garlic and onion and put to the side. Drain water from okra; add remaining ingredients. Simmer mixture for 15–20 minutes longer, until okra is tender. Add salt, if desired, to taste. Serves 4.

Onions

Without doubt the onion is the most used flavouring vegetable in the world. There is hardly a savoury dish that doesn't include onions or one of its relatives – white and red onions, garlic, chives, shallots, spring onions and leeks. Members of the onion family vary enormously in shape, size, colour, texture and intensity of flavour. Onions, particularly garlic, have also been used as medicines. The ancient Egyptians worshipped onions and during the Middle Ages they were used as currency.

Main crop onions

These are the most commonly available onions and are in the shops all year round. They are strongly flavoured, firm onions with layers of golden brown paper skins and white flesh. Generally used for cooking rather than raw. The most common varieties are Pukekohe Long Keeper and Pukekohe Early Long Keeper. As the name suggests, these store particularly well.

Pickling onions

These are simply small main crop onions. They have a strong pungent flavour. They are available all year round, but are at their best for pickling about March. To peel large quantities simply top and tail then cover with boiling water for 5 minutes, drain and remove the skins, which will slip off easily.

Red onions

These are easily recognised by their burgundy red skins and red tinged flesh. Spanish type red onions are large and round, while Californian red onions tend to be flatter and milder. The flavour is mild, sweet and juicy and they are delicious eaten raw in salads or sandwiches and as an attractive garnish. Globe shaped red onions which are normally more pungent and taste more like a main crop onion, are also becoming available. Most readily available January to August.

Shallots

Sized roughly the same or slightly larger than pickling onions, with a skin colour which ranges from coppery yellow to reddish brown. The bulbs are either elongated or oval and are formed in several clusters or bulblets. The two most commonly grown varieties are Ambition, a globe shaped bulb, and Picador, an oval shaped bulb. There is no noticeable difference in flavour.

Shallots have a more delicate, sweeter taste and finer texture than onions. They are considered the gourmet onion and are much favoured in French and Asian cooking. Delicious raw or cooked, shallots have a wide range of end uses. Shallots are available from February to July with most plentiful supply over the late summer months. They keep well in a cool dry place. In Australia, Japanese bunching onions and spring onions are often referred to as shallots.

WHAT TO LOOK FOR

Choose onions with firm flesh and dry papery outer skin. Avoid those with green shoots or soft spots.

HOW TO KEEP

Store in a cool, dark, well ventilated place. Don't put them in plastic bags. If purchased in plastic, remove from plastic as soon as possible. Don't refrigerate or store with any food which may absorb their flavour.

NUTRITIONAL VALUE

New Zealanders are big onion eaters so onions do make a significant contribution to our diets. The phytochemicals found in onions are flavonoids, fructans, sulphur-containing compounds and saponins. Evidence shows the phytochemicals in onions play an important role in protecting against major lifestyle chronic diseases as well as health problems associated with ageing. Their antimicrobial activity, long recognised in folk remedies, has also now been scientifically validated. Onions also supply a significant amount of vitamin C.

Shallots, unlike other allium species, supply a very good source of vitamin B6. Vitamin C is also present. Vitamin A is supplied as a result of carotenoids in the leaves. Shallots also provide small but useful amounts of a variety of micronutrients.

Main crop onions

Red onions

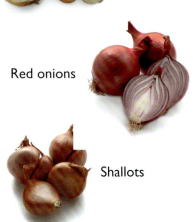

Shallots

HOW TO PREPARE

Release of the oil during peeling brings tears to the eyes – a guaranteed way of avoiding this is yet to be found. The best advice is to just go as fast as you can! Some people try putting a piece of bread between their teeth, peeling them under running water, cutting off the root or only cutting in one direction!

WAYS TO EAT THIS VEGETABLE

Onions can be eaten raw or cooked. In many recipes onions are not the main ingredient but the flavour and texture of onion makes a great contribution. They can be used in so many dishes – soups, casseroles, pizzas, pies, with pasta, in salads, sauces, chutneys, stir-fries – to name just a few! They can be prepared or cooked in many ways too – microwaved, fried, boiled, baked and roasted or pickled.

AVAILABLE TO PURCHASE

All year round.

TIPS
FOR HOME
GARDENERS

Suitable to plant: nationwide.

When to plant: spring, summer and autumn.

Approx time till harvest: 8–12 weeks.

Depth to plant: 5cm.

Spacing between rows: 20cm.

Spacing between plants: 15–20cm.

Water requirements: onions like a moist and free-draining soil.

French onion soup

You can't go past the taste and simplicity of this French classic. Rediscover how delicious and easy this soup is to make!

6 large onions, peeled and sliced

1 Tbsp oil

2 Tbsp flour

1 tsp sugar

6 cups beef or vegetable stock

Sauté the onions in the oil for 4–5 minutes or until transparent. Add the flour and sugar, mix well. Add the stock and simmer gently for 10–15 minutes or until the onion is totally softened. Serve with crusty bread or toast.

Parsnips

The parsnip is a root vegetable and belongs to the carrot family. It has a long history and has grown in Europe since Roman times. The word parsnip is from the Latin 'pastus' meaning food and 'sativa' meaning cultivated.

Parsnips have a delicate, sweet and slightly nutty flavour. Different parsnip varieties have very subtle taste variations and slightly different shapes. The sweet flavour comes about when the starch is converted to sugar. This happens in cold weather, preferably frosts. For pre-winter crops you can store parsnips at low temperatures (0°C) and there will be some starch conversion to sugar. Parsnips have become a 'trendy' vegetable and consumption is increasing. They are appreciated for their succulent and nutty taste.

WHAT TO LOOK FOR

Look for smooth and firm parsnips. Small to medium sized parsnips are the best quality, preferably around 50–70mm shoulder diameter and approximately 190–250mm in length. Avoid large coarse roots which usually have woody or fibrous centres. Different varieties are available with slightly differing shaped tapers and taste variations are marginal.

HOW TO KEEP

Refrigerate in plastic bags.

NUTRITIONAL VALUE

Parsnips are a good source of fibre and potassium and also contribute some folate, calcium, iron and magnesium. They also contain small amounts of vitamin C and E. Falcarinol, although mostly associated with carrots, is found in higher levels in parsnips.

HOW TO PREPARE

You don't need to peel young parsnips. You may need to peel or scrape the older and tougher ones. Cooking time depends on the size of the pieces and the age of the parsnip. They should be tender but still firm.

WAYS TO EAT THIS VEGETABLE

Parsnips are often served with a roast or casserole but they're also tasty in stir-fries, salads, pies, soups, souffles or cooked with potato wedges. Try strips of parsnips drizzled in olive oil and roasted with a medley of other vegetables like kumara, peppers and onions. They may be steamed, microwaved, boiled or sautéed as a side vegetable. Traditionally parsnips are boiled and mashed together with carrots. Parsnips are a favourite with home wine-makers. Parsnip cake, similar in taste and texture to carrot cake, is wonderful.

AVAILABLE TO PURCHASE

Parsnips are often thought of as a winter vegetable but are available all year round. They are sometimes a bit hard to get in summer.

Suitable to plant: nationwide.

When to plant: early spring and summer.

Approx time till harvest: 6–8 weeks.

Depth to plant: 5cm.

Spacing between rows: 20cm.

Spacing between plants: 10cm.

Water requirements: moist well-drained soil.

Parsnip and potato and rosemary wedges

Parsnips are a very popular vegetable at the moment – when you taste them roasted in garlic and rosemary like this you'll understand why! Simply delicious.

4–6 floury potatoes (800g), scrubbed and sliced into wedges

2 small parsnips, cut lengthwise into quarters

2 Tbsp flour

4 cloves garlic, peeled and finely chopped

sprinkle of sea salt (optional)

freshly ground black pepper

2 Tbsp oil

3–4 fresh rosemary sprigs

Place all ingredients in a roasting pan. Toss to coat. Bake at 200°C for 25–35 minutes or until golden brown and crunchy. Turn over several times during cooking. Garnish if desired. Remove the rosemary sprigs before serving. Serves 4.

Peas

The earliest peas to be eaten were always dried and used in winter. In the 1500s new varieties with better flavour were developed and people started eating them fresh. Since then they have always been popular. Most peas grown in New Zealand are used for processing. We tend to eat them processed a lot more than fresh because they have a relatively short season.

Snow peas

Snow peas are increasingly popular and are often used in Oriental cooking and salads. Snow peas are almost completely flat with only little bumps where the peas are inside the pod. Snow peas are also known as mange tout, which translates into English as 'eat all'. Both the seed and the pod are eaten. Differing varieties exist, some of which may be referred to as sugar peas or sugar snap peas. With some of these varieties the peas are more developed before harvesting.

WHAT TO LOOK FOR

Look for firm bright green pods which are not too full. Snow peas should have very small peas in the pod and be roughly the same size.
Buy small quantities regularly. Whilst peas will keep for about a week, they taste a lot better when eaten in one to two days. Once picked the sugars naturally present in the peas are converted to starches, hence the fresher the pea the sweeter it will be.

HOW TO KEEP

Refrigerate in plastic bags and use as soon as possible.

NUTRITIONAL VALUE

Peas are very good for you, providing an excellent source of fibre and they are one of the best vegetable sources of protein. They are a good source of vitamin C, folate and thiamine, as well as vitamins B6, B3 and B2. They also contain a range of minerals, notably iron and copper, with some phosphorus, potassium, zinc and magnesium. The major phytochemicals in peas are the carotenoids, including lutein and zeaxanthin and β-carotene, phenolics compounds, including some flavonoids as well as phenolic acids.
Snow peas have more vitamin C, but less fibre and protein. They supply good levels of carotenoids and useful amounts of vitamins B1 and B6, iron and folate.

HOW TO PREPARE

The fresher the pea, the better and sweeter the taste. Use them as soon as possible after you buy them and don't overcook them. Peas should be shelled just before you eat them. You can top and tail snow peas but depending on your end use, this is not always necessary.

WAYS TO EAT THIS VEGETABLE

Fresh peas are delicious steamed or boiled, perhaps with a little mint. They can also be used to make soup or puréed and served with meats. Snow peas need to be cooked just lightly until they are tender but still crisp. They are often used in stir-fries. Both peas and snow peas are great in salads, either raw or cooked.

AVAILABLE TO PURCHASE

You can buy peas from November until February, but even in season the supply is limited. Snow peas are more readily available than peas and can be obtained from October until April with a limited supply in May, June and September.

TIPS
FOR HOME
GARDENERS

Suitable to plant: nationwide.

When to plant: early spring in frost-free areas and summer.

Approx time till harvest: 4–6 weeks.

Depth to plant: 5cm.

Spacing between rows: 40–50cm depending on the height of the variety planted.

Spacing between plants: 10cm.

Water requirements: ample water produces the best pea crops.

Cherry tomato salad

Delightfully simple and very elegant.

2 cups snow peas

3 cups cherry tomatoes

1 packet cress sprouts

1–2 shallots, finely chopped

1 Tbsp lemon juice

1 Tbsp olive oil

2 tsp sugar

freshly ground black pepper

Blanch the snow peas in boiling water for 2–3 minutes until bright green and still a little crunchy. Drain and quickly cool under cold running water to prevent further cooking. Scatter with the cherry tomatoes on your serving platter. Snip the cress sprouts and add to the salad in little bunches. Place the shallots, lemon juice, oil and sugar in a screw top jar and shake vigorously until the sugar has dissolved. Drizzle over the salad, season with pepper if desired. Serves 4.

Potatoes

Potatoes, often called spuds, are probably native to the Andes in South America. They have been a staple food of the Europeans and North Americans for nearly two hundred years. It's the swollen underground stem we eat, called a tuber. Potatoes, like most of the common vegetables we know today, came to New Zealand from the British Isles and were established by 1880 as a staple part of the early settlers' diet.

There is a lot of interest in different potato varieties. The often large differences in texture, flavour and shape make each variety suitable to its own particular method of cooking. There are many grown in New Zealand, but there are about 10 to 12 varieties which are predominant and readily available. In addition there are a lot of varieties which have limited and/or localised supplies.

Potatoes are the most popular vegetable in New Zealand with 97% of us eating them. 53% of New Zealanders consume fresh potatoes four times per week and 21% of New Zealanders eat them daily.

WHAT TO LOOK FOR

Choose potatoes that haven't got any cuts, bruises, green patches or shoots. Sometimes you may choose a smooth looking potato over a misshapen one and assume that it is a better product. This is not necessarily the case as some varieties characteristically have skins which are netted or have eyes in them. A potato does not have to look good to cook brilliantly! Different potatoes will cook differently – so you need to use a potato suited to your end use. However, even the same variety will sometimes cook differently.

Buy potatoes by end use. These potatoes will have been cook tested by the growers or packers and will cook according to the packaging. They will be marked as for 'boiling', 'salads', 'wedges' or 'baking', for example. For best results select the right potato for the job. If a potato does not perform how you predicted, you need to be prepared to change your cooking method to match the type of potato you have.

At either ends of the spectrum, a potato is either 'floury' or 'waxy'. Some potatoes are less floury or less waxy than others. These potatoes fall in the area of 'general-purpose' and will tend to perform most tasks, although perhaps with not as good results as the ones which clearly fall into the floury or waxy category.

As the season progresses, potatoes change – for example, an Ilam Hardy early in the season (October) is quite waxy. As the Ilam Hardy gets older it is a good general-purpose potato, whilst towards the end of the season when a lot more of the natural sugars have converted to starch, it tends to be floury. Not all potatoes show such a range of characteristics.

Weather, climate and soil have a dramatic effect on the cooking performance of a potato. For example, a Southland grown Nadine may be very waxy whilst a Pukekohe grown Nadine may be only slightly waxy. The flavour is also influenced.

HOW TO KEEP

Store them in a well ventilated cool dark place. Don't put them in the fridge as the flavour changes will be noticeable. Remove them from plastic packaging, unless it is a 'Greenguard' bag, manufactured specifically for potatoes. Place them gently in your storage area because even though they look tough they do bruise easily. A heavy paper bag or cardboard box makes a good storage container.

When potatoes are exposed to light they can develop a green colour resulting in chlorophyll formation in the surface layers. Associated with this is the formation of a toxic alkaloid, solanine. The amount of green pigment depends on the intensity of the light, length of exposure and age of potato. New potatoes are really susceptible to greening. Some varieties have quite a yellow flesh so don't confuse this with greening. If you do purchase potatoes with lots of greening, return them to your retailer. If there are small amounts of greening simply peel or scrape away the greening and use the potato normally.

Natural dirt and dust on potatoes can help to keep them fresher so it is best not to wash them until you are ready to cook them — or if you buy ready washed, buy small quantities regularly.

NUTRITIONAL VALUE

The potato has been described as the phytochemical jewel box. They are a great fuel food to power your body and provide a wealth of nutrients, especially vitamin C and potassium. Vitamin C in potatoes is very important as we eat so many potatoes, for example New Zealanders get around 30% of their vitamin C requirement from potatoes. They are a valuable source of B group vitamins, particularly B6, thiamin and niacin. Potatoes are also a good source of fibre and they contain some iron and magnesium. They are high in starch so will stop you feeling hungry for a long time. Antioxidants present in potatoes are phenolic acids, vitamin C and in yellow fleshed or red skinned varieties –

Mediterranean mash

Comfort food at its best - mashed potatoes reign supreme in terms of taste, texture and just making all meals better! This particular mash is no exception!

4 large floury potatoes (900g)

¼– ½ cup milk

2 Tbsp olive oil

½ cup caper berries or olives

¼ cup sliced sun-dried tomatoes

¼ cup marinated feta cheese

¼ cup finely chopped fresh parsley or chives

freshly ground black pepper

Peel the potatoes and cut into even-sized pieces. Boil for 25–35 minutes or until soft. Drain. Mash in the milk and oil, adding extra milk if necessary to make the potatoes smooth and creamy. Mix in the caper berries, sun-dried tomatoes, feta and herbs. Season with pepper.

carotenoids and anthocyanins respectively. Potatoes are also a source of high quality protein.

Potatoes are not fattening, however some cooking and preparation methods are!

HOW TO PREPARE

When possible, don't peel your potato as most of the antioxidants and fibre are just under the skin. Leaving the skin on will also help prevent water soluble vitamins leaching out during cooking. Simply wash and scrub it. Any green areas should be discarded.

WAYS TO EAT THIS VEGETABLE

There are many ways to cook potatoes – the serving suggestions are endless! You can eat them baked, mashed, boiled, sautéed, scalloped, as wedges, potato skins, roasted or fried, added to soups, in salads.

AVAILABLE TO PURCHASE

All year round. You can buy new season potatoes from late August until February.

TIPS
FOR HOME
GARDENERS

Suitable to plant: nationwide.

When to plant: depending on the variety, from early spring until mid summer.

Approx time till harvest: 8–10 weeks.

Depth to plant: 15cm.

Spacing between rows: 40cm.

Spacing between plants: 40cm.

Water requirements: water regularly during hot dry weather.

Different types of potatoes

Waxy
most 'early' new season varieties
These potatoes tend to be waxy and are ideal for boiling, salads, casseroles, soups.

Draga   Nadine   Frisia

And limited or localised supplies of Jersey Bennie, Liseta, Red King Edward, Tiffany.

Waxy/floury
These potatoes tend to be general-purpose making them suitable for most end uses.

Rua   Desiree   Karaka   Moonlight

And limited or localised supplies of Red Ruby, Rocket, Maris Anchor.

Floury
These potatoes tend to be floury and are ideal for mashing, wedges, chips, roasting, baking.

Ilam Hardy   Red Rascal   Agria   Fianna

And limited or localised supplies of White Delight.

Puha

Puha or Rauriki is a green vegetable native to New Zealand. It was one of the staple green vegetables of Māori and is still eaten today. Puha can be found growing wild. The 'smooth' leaved puha is the most popular. The slightly bitter and 'prickly' leaved puha is also eaten. Whilst it is not grown commercially it is occasionally available and there is certainly demand for it in some areas.

WHAT TO LOOK FOR
Select young and crisp puha with a good even colouring.

HOW TO KEEP
Refrigerate in plastic bags and use promptly. Puha can be frozen but it is best fresh.

NUTRITIONAL VALUE
Puha provides a very good source of iron, fibre, vitamin A and C.

HOW TO PREPARE
Rub the stems and leaves together under running water and then steam or boil them like spinach. You may need to cook them for 20 to 30 minutes to remove the bitterness.

WAYS TO EAT THIS VEGETABLE
It is common practice to boil puha with meat. It is placed on top of roast beef, pork or mutton bird for 15–20 minutes before the end of cooking. Puha can also be used as a vegetable on its own or in a meat or vegetable casserole or in salads. You can use it to make soup, add it to a rice stir-fry or put it in pies.

AVAILABLE TO PURCHASE
Puha grows all year round but is not often available commercially.

Puha and bacon

6 handfuls of puha

3 rashers of lean bacon, sliced

Wash puha thoroughly. Unless the plants are very young and tender, squeeze or rub stalks. This gets rid of the more bitter taste of the milky juices in the stems of the older plants. Place a saucepan of water on to boil. When boiling, add the puha and bacon gradually so that the water keeps boiling. Stir every five minutes. Boil uncovered for 30 minutes. Serves 4 as a side vegetable.

TIPS
FOR HOME
GARDENERS

Suitable to plant: nationwide in warm sheltered gardens.

When to plant: spring and summer.

Approx time till harvest: 4–6 weeks.

Depth to plant: 5cm.

Spacing between rows: 30cm.

Spacing between plants: 30cm.

Water requirements: puha grows best in a rich, moist soil.

Pumpkins & winter squash

Thought to have originated in South America, pumpkins have been enjoyed for centuries. Māori ate gourds baked in the hangi before Europeans came.

The terms pumpkin and squash are often used interchangeably. Pumpkin generally describes winter squash which are hard skinned, hard fleshed mature fruit. By contrast summer squash are soft skinned and include marrow, courgette (or zucchini) and scallopini.

There are lots of different varieties available and whilst they vary in taste and texture, most can be used interchangeably in recipes. Like most vegetables, there is sometimes enormous variation between characteristics of a specific type of pumpkin or squash. This is caused by variations in growing conditions such as temperature, soil type and fertiliser used. Hence a buttercup squash grown at Pukekohe may taste significantly different from the same variety grown in Marlborough. Similarly, pumpkins grown in the same area may taste different each season.

WHAT TO LOOK FOR

Choose firm pumpkins and squash that have undamaged skin and feel heavy for their size. It is important to select pumpkin and squash which are mature. A mature pumpkin or squash will be shiny or slightly slippery to feel, whilst an immature one will be slightly sticky. Another indication is brown flecks (or corking) on the stem. The more flecks the more mature.

HOW TO KEEP

Store in a cool, dark, dry place. Once cut, remove the seeds, wrap in plastic film and refrigerate.

NUTRITIONAL VALUE

Pumpkins and squash are an excellent source of vitamin A, containing high levels of the provitamin A carotenes (α-carotene, β-carotene, β-cryptoxanthin) which the body converts to vitamin A. Lutein and zeaxanthin are also found. The brighter and stronger the colour of the flesh, the more carotenoids the pumpkin will contain. Some vitamin C, potassium and fibre are also supplied in useful amounts. Pumpkin is surprisingly low in calories, containing less than vegetables of similar texture like kumara, parsnip and potatoes.

HOW TO PREPARE

Pumpkin and squash are interchangeable and can be used in the same recipes. Some varieties have very tough skins which are difficult to cut. Often it is easier to cook the pumpkin with the skin on and then remove the flesh. This is easy in the microwave. If they are whole pierce the skin well before you cook them, otherwise they'll explode. Alternatively, roughly chop and boil or microwave the pieces until tender.

WAYS TO EAT THIS VEGETABLE

Traditionally roasted, pumpkin can also be used in soups, flans and pies. It can also be baked and stuffed, and made into moist cakes and breads. Baked, steamed, sautéed, steamed or mashed, pumpkin makes a delicious side vegetable and is particularly enhanced by nutmeg. Cooked and cooled it is also good in a salad.

AVAILABLE TO PURCHASE

All year round depending on the variety.

Buttercup squash

They have dark rich green hard skin with speckles and stripes and a round flat shape. Generally 15–20cm in diameter and about 1.5kg, they have a fine textured orange to dark yellow flesh with a slightly sweet flavour. Immature buttercups will have a paler flesh. The skin is softer than other pumpkin or squash types and hence they have a shorter shelf life.

Crown or grey

They have a hard blue/grey skin, with a rich orange flesh. Crown pumpkins are generally 30cm in diameter, 10cm deep, and about 4kg. The most commonly sold crown in New Zealand is Whangaparoa. Because of their hard skin they keep well and are usually available all year round.

Halloween

These pumpkins have a bright orange skin which is very hard and knobby. The flesh is very dense and is deep orange in colour. The most common variety is Red Warren.

Spaghetti squash

Pale yellow skin about 20–30cm long with a light yellow flesh. Either bake whole or cut into quarters and steam. Once cooked, spaghetti squash can be scooped out and incorporated into recipes and used like pasta. Spaghetti squash have limited availability and are generally available in the early months of the year.

Butternut

They have a creamy beige skin and have an elongated cylindrical shape. They have orange flesh and a sweet flavour. Flavour varies with variety, growing conditions and season.

Mini squash or yumpkins

These are small and can have green, yellow or orange skins. Supply, though all year round, is limited with a better supply in the north. There are many varieties of small squash which are increasing in popularity. Each has slightly different characteristics and flavour. Varieties include sun drop, orange minikin, red hub, sunset squash, sweet mischief, and white acorn. Mini squash have also become popular for decorative purposes – coated with polyurethane, they will last a long time in an arrangement.

Kumi kumi

Kumi kumi are stocky in shape with heavy ribbing. Immature kumi kumi are about the size of a tennis ball, have a nutty flavour, a speckled green soft skin with white-green flesh and are used like courgettes. Mature kumi kumi have a speckled green hard skin, are about the size of a netball, have a deep white flesh and are used like buttercup squash. Originally called kamo kamo by Māori and considered particularly good for the hangi. Available December to April.

Pumpkin with orange

This sweet citrus sauce over pumpkins is fantastic. It is great on other vegetables too – parsnip, carrot, swede, kumara, turnip, pumpkin or yam – either by themselves or as a mixture.

500g pumpkin, peeled, seeds removed and cut into wedges

1 Tbsp brown sugar

1 Tbsp butter

1 tsp grated orange rind

2 Tbsp orange juice

freshly ground black pepper

2 Tbsp toasted pinenuts

2 Tbsp finely chopped fresh herbs e.g. chives

Place the vegetables, brown sugar, butter, rind, juice and pepper in a microwave-proof dish. Mix, cover and cook on high power for 6–8 minutes or until tender. Stir once during cooking. Mix the herbs and pinenuts through the vegetables. Serves 4.

TIPS
FOR HOME
GARDENERS

Suitable to plant: nationwide in warm sheltered gardens.

When to plant: spring and summer.

Approx time till harvest: 10–12 weeks.

Depth to plant: 5cm.

Spacing between rows: 40cm.

Spacing between plants: 60cm.

Water requirements: water well when fruit is forming.

Radishes

The name 'radish' is derived from the Latin words 'radix' meaning root, and 'raphanus' meaning easily grown. However radish is really a swollen stem rather than a root even though it grows underground! Thought to be a native of Asia, there are many varieties of radish which vary in size, shape, flavour and colour. Radishes were once thought to be an antidote for mushroom poisoning and to have many medicinal uses.

Red radish

The most common radishes in New Zealand are the red varieties, either globe shaped or slightly cylindrical.

Daikon radish

(Japanese radish, giant radish, Chinese radish, Lo Baak, Lo Bok)

The Daikon radish is growing in popularity here. It is a large radish about 5cm in diameter and up to 40cm long. It is used both raw and cooked and may be sliced, chopped, grated or cut into match sticks for salads, dipping sauces, marinades and soups. It can be parboiled and then treated as a turnip. It may also be pickled or dried. Often it is carved as a decorative garnish.

WHAT TO LOOK FOR
Firm flesh with a bright colour and a smooth, unblemished skin. Leaves, if they're still attached, should be fresh, green and not wilted. Avoid oversized red radishes as these can be woody or pulpy.

HOW TO KEEP
Remove tops and refrigerate in a plastic bag. Use promptly.

NUTRITIONAL VALUE
On a per weight basis compared with other vegetables, radishes have high levels of vitamin C. They also contain some fibre, potassium and folate but, like many salad vegetables, they are high in water and so are not nutrient dense. The peppery taste of radishes is evidence of the presence of the phytochemicals glucosinolates and isothiocyanates. Anthocyanins are present.

HOW TO PREPARE
Just cut the green off if it's still attached and wash. Trim the thin tip of the root.

WAYS TO EAT THIS VEGETABLE
Red radishes are mainly used raw in salads or as a garnish. White radishes may be eaten raw or boiled, baked or used in Asian cooking and in pickles.

AVAILABLE TO PURCHASE
All year round.

Raw vegetable platter

Sweet Chilli Dipping Sauce

This light sauce is perfect with a range of fresh or lightly blanched vegetables. Radishes, carrots and snow peas are wonderful with this.

¼ cup white vinegar	½ medium carrot, finely chopped
½ cup sugar	¼ small green cucumber, seeded and finely chopped
2 Tbsp water	
1 small red chilli, deseeded and finely sliced (or Thai Style chilli sauce to taste)	4–6 radishes, finely chopped

Combine the vinegar, sugar, water and chilli in a pan. Bring to the boil, stirring until the sugar is dissolved. Boil uncovered for 3 minutes . Pour syrup over the vegetables. Serve warm or cold.

TIPS
FOR HOME
GARDENERS

Suitable to plant: nationwide.

When to plant: year round.

Approx time till harvest: 2–4 weeks.

Depth to plant: shallowly at 2–3cm.

Spacing between rows: 10cm.

Spacing between plants: 3cm.

Water requirements: water regularly.

Rhubarb

You probably think of rhubarb as a fruit because it's usually eaten as a dessert, but it's actually a vegetable. Thought to be a native of Tibet, rhubarb is the leaf stalk or petiole of a perennial plant.

WHAT TO LOOK FOR
Look for firm, red glossy stalks which are crisp and showing no signs of wilting.

HOW TO KEEP
Refrigerate in plastic bags.

NUTRITIONAL VALUE
Rhubarb is a good source of fibre, potassium and calcium. It also provides some vitamin C.

HOW TO PREPARE
Young rhubarb stalks need to be washed and cut into pieces. Older, thicker rhubarb needs any coarse strings removed before slicing. Don't eat the leaves as they are poisonous.

WAYS TO EAT THIS VEGETABLE
Rhubarb stewed with a little sugar is great added to your breakfast cereal, or eaten with ice-cream as a dessert. It tastes great in muffins, cakes, jams, flans or in crumbles (in place of or in addition to apples).

AVAILABLE TO PURCHASE
Rhubarb is available all year round and is at its best from May until October.

Stewed rhubarb

Stewed rhubarb is fantastic with your favourite breakfast cereal. It will keep in the fridge for several days.

8–10 stalks rhubarb (300g)

1¼ cups water

¼ cup sugar

Chop the rhubarb stalks into 3cm lengths. Place the rhubarb, water and sugar in a saucepan. Cover and simmer for 6–8 minutes or until softened.

TIPS
FOR HOME
GARDENERS

Suitable to plant: nationwide.

When to plant: spring and early summer.

Approx time till harvest: 8–12 weeks.

Depth to plant: 10–15cm.

Spacing between rows: 40cm.

Spacing between plants: 40cm.

Water requirements: rhubarb grows best in a moist well-drained soil.

Mesclun

Mesclun is the French term given to a mixture of tender young gourmet salad greens. Mesclun contains combinations of salad leaves; in addition it may also include lettuces and herbs. Leaves included in a mesclun mix will vary with time of year and from brand to brand.

Salad greens

Besides lettuce there is a vast array of other leaves, often loosely termed 'salad greens'. Whilst some have been around for a while and are sold separately, like rocket and watercress, there is a range of stunning leaves and these are usually sold in mixes with other leaves.

Baby spinach

Young spinach leaves are often used in salad mixes and sold with other salad greens. Baby spinach has juicy, ruffled leaves with a mild spinach flavour. Spinach is particularly nutrient dense with a wide range of health benefits.

Tat soi

This is an Asian cabbage which is used when very young in salads of all kinds. It has a very mild cabbage flavour.

Red mustard

These young leaves have a faint sharp mustard flavour and are especially good with mizuna and other young leaves. The small leaves, whilst being predominantly red on the upper-side, have green colouring on the under-side.

Pea shoots (dau miu)

These are the tender tips off young pea shoots. They are sweet and succulent.

Red chard

These young leaves are green with red veins. They have a faint beet-like flavour and are especially good in warm salads.

Green mustard

Like the red mustard, there are many different varieties of mustard available and leaf shape varies considerably. Flavour also varies from mild to intense.

Rocket

Standard rocket

Wild rocket (roquette, arugula)
There are two main varieties grown commercially – standard rocket and wild rocket. Wild rocket is growing rapidly in popularity and is more common than the standard variety. It has a stronger flavour than the standard rocket. As shown, wild rocket looks totally different from standard rocket. Wild rocket has dark green deeply lobed leaves and has a spicy piquant flavour. It is ideal to mix with other lettuce leaves and commonly found in commercially available lettuce leaf mixes.

Mizuna

Like rocket, mizuna has a spicy piquant flavour, is great mixed with other lettuce leaves and is commonly found in commercially available lettuce leaf mixes. Mizuna is a medium green with deeply jagged leaves. Mibuna, another salad green, is very similar but has a slightly stronger flavouring.

Mibuna

A very similar leaf, in both appearance and taste, to mizuna but has a slightly stronger flavouring.

Frisee

Blanched leaves of finely curled endive. It is slightly bitter and provides an attractive 'coral' appearance in mesclun mixes.

Lambs lettuce

(corn salad, mache)

Lambs lettuce is very succulent with a delicate flavour and smoothly textured green leaves.

Watercress

See Watercress.

WHAT TO LOOK FOR

Choose clean, crisp leaves.

HOW TO KEEP

Refrigerate in plastic bags or in the crisper. Make sure the leaves aren't squashed. Use promptly.

NUTRITIONAL VALUE

Both core nutrients and phytochemicals abound in a mesclun mix of leaves. The variation in the mixes provides a range of phytonutrients including high levels of vitamin A, anthocyanins and glucosinolates /isothiocyanates.

HOW TO PREPARE

Remove any coarse or wilted leaves. If the leaves get a little limp you can easily revive them. Simply soak the leaves in warm water for 3–4 minutes. Cover and refrigerate for about 20 minutes. The results are very impressive and you will be surprised how crisp the leaves will become.

WAYS TO EAT THIS VEGETABLE

Salad greens are mostly used raw in salads or as garnishing. Experiment as several of the varieties taste good when lightly blanched and served in a warm salad.

AVAILABLE TO PURCHASE

As most of these new varieties are grown indoors, they are available all year round. In some areas supply is limited.

Peppers and baby onions

No matter what time of year, or if you are serving this with hot or cold foods, this salad works so well and tastes fabulous!

2 yellow peppers, cut into wedges

6 baby onions, peeled and halved

olive oil for spraying

8–10 cherry tomatoes, halved

1 avocado, sliced

5 handfuls mesclun

2–3 Tbsp vinaigrette e.g. herb

Place the peppers and onions on an oven tray. Spray with olive oil. Bake at 200°C for 20–25 minutes. Allow to cool slightly on a serving platter and add the rest of the ingredients. Toss the vinaigrette through the salad. Serves 4.

Choose crisp green leaves with firm white stalks. Avoid leaves which are wilted or damaged.

HOW TO KEEP

Refrigerate in plastic bags. Use promptly.

NUTRITIONAL VALUE

Silver beet is an excellent source of vitamin C and E and provitamin A (β-carotene) and like its cousin, spinach, is also rich in vitamin B6, folate, and contains a wide range of minerals including iron. It has very high levels of various antioxidants including the carotenoids, lutein and zeaxanthin and the flavonoids kaempferol and quercetin.

HOW TO PREPARE

When cooking leaves, don't add water as the water that clings to them after washing is sufficient. The stems can be stripped off and cooked like asparagus. Alternatively both the stems and leaves can be used together. The stems take longer to cook so add the leaves 3–4 minutes after the stems. Silver beet suits quick cooking methods like stir-frying, steaming or microwaving.

WAYS TO EAT THIS VEGETABLE

The young leaves can be used raw in a salad but silver beet is usually eaten cooked. Puréed or finely chopped silver beet makes an excellent base for many dishes including roulard, pies, quiches or omelettes.

AVAILABLE TO PURCHASE

All year round.

Silver beet

The Greeks were the first to regard silver beet as a food. Later the Romans considered it a delicacy. It's also known as chard, Swiss chard and seakale beet. Regarded as similar to spinach, silver beet has a stronger flavour. The main variety of silver beet has a white stalk. Red beet is sometimes available. It has the same green leaves but has a rich pinky-red stem and veins. Silver beet grows all year round and is easy to cultivate – hence it is a favourite of home gardeners.

Suitable to plant: nationwide in frost-free gardens.

When to plant: spring until autumn.

Approx time till harvest: 6–8 weeks.

Depth to plant: 5cm.

Spacing between rows: 30cm.

Spacing between plants: 30cm.

Water requirements: moist well-drained soil grows the best silver beet.

Vegetable slice

A great variety of different vegetables can be used in this Vegetable slice.

3 cups seasonal vegetables e.g. finely chopped onion, pepper or tomato, grated carrot or courgette, finely sliced mushrooms, beans or asparagus, cooked and drained spinach or silver beet

1 cup grated tasty cheese

4 eggs

¾ cup milk

½ cup self-raising flour

2 rashers lean bacon, finely chopped (optional)

freshly ground black pepper

Place the vegetables and cheese in a well-greased baking dish. Lightly beat the eggs and milk together. Sprinkle over the self-raising flour and mix well, ensuring there are no lumps. Pour over the vegetables. Top with bacon and pepper. Bake at 200°C for 30–35 minutes or until golden brown and set. Serve either hot or cold. Serves 5.

Spinach

Spinach was made famous last century by Popeye the Sailor when eating spinach made his muscles bulge. However, spinach has been around for a lot longer than that. It originated in Asia and was introduced to Europe by Arab traders during the 13th century.

When cooked and chopped, the taste is often confused with silver beet. However, spinach has a milder flavour. Spinach and silver beet can be used in the same recipes, although spinach has become the preferred option, with rising consumption in New Zealand.

Baby spinach

Young spinach leaves are often used in salad mixes and sold with other salad greens. Baby spinach has juicy ruffled leaves with a mild spinach flavour. New Zealand spinach is a native that grows wild, has triangular leaves and trails over the ground. It is generally cooked as the leaves are coarse and slightly furry when raw. The flavour is similar to standard spinach.

WHAT TO LOOK FOR
Choose crisp green leaves with no signs of wilting or blemishes.

HOW TO KEEP
Refrigerate in plastic bags. Use promptly.

NUTRITIONAL VALUE
Spinach fully deserves its reputation as a health-enhancing vegetable, being rich in both core nutrients and phytochemicals. The major nutrients in spinach are pro vitamin A (in the form of β-carotene), vitamins C, K and folate and the minerals, calcium, iron and potassium. Spinach also provides fibre and has the additional advantage of being low in calories. The phytochemicals of most importance are the carotenoids, β-carotene, lutein and zeaxanthin and phenolic compounds.

HOW TO PREPARE
Spinach should be cooked without added water. The water that clings to the spinach after washing should be enough. It suits quick cooking methods such as steaming, boiling, stir-frying or microwaving. Remove the stems only if you are eating it raw. Otherwise slice and cook with the leaves. On cooking spinach condenses a lot, so you do need to use a lot of raw leaves in order to yield enough when cooked.

WAYS TO EAT THIS VEGETABLE
Spinach is very versatile. It can be used in many ways including raw in salads, cooked in a soufflé, omelette, quiche, paté, pancake filling, soup, or as a sauce on pasta.

AVAILABLE TO PURCHASE
All year round.

Suitable to plant: nationwide in warm sheltered gardens.

When to plant: spring and summer.

Approx time till harvest: 6–8 weeks.

Depth to plant: 5cm.

Spacing between rows: 30cm.

Spacing between plants: 20cm.

Water requirements: water at least twice a week when plants are growing vigorously.

Parsnips with baby spinach

3 medium parsnips, cut into thin sticks

1 tsp coriander seeds

2 tsp mustard seeds

olive oil for spraying

8–10 cherry tomatoes, halved

5 handfuls baby spinach

2–3 Tbsp vinaigrette e.g. balsamic

Place the parsnips, coriander and mustard seeds on an oven tray. Spray with olive oil. Bake at 200°C for 20–25 minutes. Allow to cool slightly on a serving platter and add the rest of the ingredients. Toss the vinaigrette through the salad. Serves 4.

Spring onions

Spring onions belong to the onion family. In some countries they are known as scallions, bunching or green onions. They are milder than onions, which makes them ideal for eating raw and using in salads. The green tops of spring onions are often used like chives, as a garnish or cut up in salads.

These small white onions are harvested when young and green before the bulb has time to form properly. Tender and mild with a long white slender neck and hollow green tops, they are sold fresh in bunches.

WHAT TO LOOK FOR
Look for solid white bulbs with white root hairs firmly attached, and crisp, bright green stems.

HOW TO KEEP
Refrigerate in plastic bags in the crisper.

NUTRITIONAL VALUE
Spring onions are a good source of fibre and calcium. They provide high levels of vitamin C as well as potassium. They also supply carotenoids and chlorophyll.

HOW TO PREPARE
Cut the root off and the tips of the stems if they are damaged.

WAYS TO EAT THIS VEGETABLE
The entire onion, including the top is used raw in salads, sauces, as a garnish, or in a multitude of quick cooking methods – hence their popularity in Oriental cooking. Cut the green tops finely and use like chives. The mild taste of spring onions makes them ideal stirred into a sauce to be poured over poultry, meat, pasta or other vegetables.

AVAILABLE TO PURCHASE
Available all year round with a shorter supply in mid-winter.

TIPS
FOR HOME
GARDENERS

Suitable to plant: nationwide in sheltered gardens.

When to plant: spring through late summer.

Approx time till harvest: 6–8 weeks.

Depth to plant: 5cm.

Spacing between rows: 20cm.

Spacing between plants: 5cm.

Water requirements: keep the soil moist at all times.

Fruity watercress and chicken salad

Fresh and absolutely delicious!

8–10 lettuce leaves (iceberg)

2 cups watercress sprigs

1 cup crunchy sprouts

3 spring onions, sliced

2 cups chopped and sliced cucumber

2 cups prepared fruits, e.g. halved strawberries, chunks of melon, pawpaw, persimmon or kiwifruit

1 cup sliced smoked chicken

Dressing

¼ cup lemon or lime juice

¼ cup light olive oil

2 Tbsp sugar

freshly ground black pepper

Arrange the lettuce and watercress onto serving plates. Top with the sprouts, spring onion, cucumber, fruit and chicken. Blend the lemon juice, oil, sugar and pepper together until the sugar dissolves, pour over salad. Serves 4.

Sprouted beans & seeds

Bean sprouts have been cultivated in Asia for thousands of years and were brought to New Zealand with the first Asian immigrants in Gold Rush days. Sprouts were made popular with the hippie movement in the States in the seventies and have only been available commercially in New Zealand since 1981.

Sprouts start as dry beans and seeds. They are sprouted by first soaking in water, then draining. Once wet, they draw on their stored nutrients and begin to grow. Being young, most sprouts are sweet and tender and provide interesting textures, being crunchy rather than fibrous like older plants. Many different sprouts are available and they are often sold in combination packs.

WHAT TO LOOK FOR
Look for fresh, crisp sprouts which are free of moisture. Avoid any with brown or grey discoloration on the shoots.

HOW TO KEEP
Refrigerate in a well-vented plastic container or bag. Sprouted beans and seeds are nearly always packaged in a special snap-top plastic container. Keep it closed in the fridge so the sprouts don't dry out. Correctly stored the sprouts will last:
Alfalfa (and alfalfa mixtures), peas, snow peas: 10–14 days.
Adzuki, baby mung, lentils, chick pea: 7–10 days.
Chinese mung bean sprouts: 5–7 days.

NUTRITIONAL VALUE
The major nutrients in sprouted beans and seeds are the B group vitamins, particularly thiamin. They also provide large amounts of a range of minerals, especially copper and zinc. Some, such as alfalfa and pea shoots, have high water content and thus have low concentrations of the nutrients they supply, but are also low in calories. Some, such as adzuki, contain more dry matter, higher nutrient levels, but more calories.

HOW TO PREPARE
There's no preparation. Rinse in water, eat and enjoy!

WAYS TO EAT THIS VEGETABLE
Bean sprouts are used a lot in Oriental cooking, salads and sandwiches. They are also good in omelettes or as edible garnishes. Bean sprouts and sprouted seeds can be used wherever you would use lettuce.

AVAILABLE TO PURCHASE
All year round.

Alfalfa and alfalfa sprout mixtures

Alfalfa is by far the most popular sprout in New Zealand. In Arabic it means 'father of all foods'. Alfalfa sprouts have a fresh crisp taste and are often combined with other flavours such as radish and onion. Yellowish alfalfa doesn't mean that it is old; the leaves have not been exposed to much light and the green chlorophyll has not yet developed. If the leaves are green, they've probably been under a fluorescent light for more than two days. Alfalfa sprouts are almost always used raw.

Adzuki sprouts (aduki sprouts)

They are small and reddish-brown with short white shoots with no leaves. They have a nutty taste and can be eaten raw and cooked. Use them in salads as you would any nuts.

Mung bean sprouts
(Chinese mung beans)

They have long shoots of 3–5cm and the coat on the mung bean is a very pale green-yellow. They can be used cooked or raw. They are very often used in stir-fries.

Snow pea shoots

These have the characteristic taste of snow peas and have long white shoots about 5–7cm long. They are used raw in salads and sandwiches. They should be crisp and firm with no signs of browning.

Baby mung sprouts

These are mung bean shoots with only a small white root and they still have an olive green coat on the bean. They are eaten raw and cooked.

Lentil sprouts

They are small, flat and blue-grey or light brown coloured seeds with a short shoot. They are crunchy and have a nutty taste. They can be used cooked or raw.

Blue pea sprouts

They are blue-green peas with a short white sprout. The peas are crunchy with a strong but tasty pea flavour.

Broccoli sprouts

These look very similar to alfalfa, but have a stronger flavour. They are sometimes sold in mixes with other sprouts, like red cabbage sprouts.

Chick pea sprouts

These are a large white pea with a creamy nutty flavour. Ideal in Mediterranean dishes such as the blended base for hummus.

Radish sprouts

These have a very distinctive hot and peppery radish flavour. They are often sold mixed with other sprouts, and may be either red or green varieties.

Popcorn shoots

These long, thin, white-stemmed, yellow-leaved sprouts have an unmistakeable sweet buttery popcorn taste.

TIPS
FOR HOME
GARDENERS

Suitable to plant: nationwide.

When to plant: year round.

Approx time till harvest: 10–12 days.

Water requirements: keep moist at all times.

No cook noodles

This is great for serious after school munchies and sure to impress your mates (and your Mum!)

2 cups boiling water

1 packet 2 minute noodles

1 ½ cups mung bean sprouts

½ cup grated carrot

½ cup grated courgette

1 Tbsp Hoisin sauce

Pour the boiling water over the noodles, mung shoots, carrot and courgette. Allow to sit for 5 minutes. Drain well. Gently toss in the Hoisin sauce. Serves 4 as a snack, or 2 as a light meal.

Swedes

Swedes belong to the same family as turnips and cabbages. They have been around since the 17th century when the swede was developed, in Sweden, from a hybrid between a turnip and a type of cabbage. Different cultures have developed their own ways to use them. The Scottish serve them boiled and mashed with their traditional dish, haggis. In the American Midwest they are mashed and candied and in Finland they are casseroled with cream and spices. Swede is also known as Swedish turnip or rutabaga. 'Rutabaga' is Swedish for red bags, referring to the purple, bronze crowns.

Whilst quite similar to turnips, swede flesh is yellow-orange, not white, and they taste sweeter than turnips. They are more available in winter and are said to be better tasting after a good frost, hence the best swedes in New Zealand are reputed to be those grown south of Gore in Southland.

Although the leaves are eaten in many countries, it's the edible roots that are commercially available in New Zealand. Swedes have a delicate flavour, a great texture and are very versatile.

WHAT TO LOOK FOR
Choose smaller swedes, about the size of a cricket ball, with a smooth skin and firm flesh.

HOW TO KEEP
Refrigerate in plastic bags.

NUTRITIONAL VALUE
Swedes are a good source of fibre and a reasonable source of calcium and vitamins A and C. Swedes are a member of the brassica family and contain many phytochemicals, particularly the phytosterols and glucosinolates.

HOW TO PREPARE
You don't always have to peel swedes. If they are fresh and young, leave the skin on.

WAYS TO EAT THIS VEGETABLE
Young swedes are crisp like an apple and can be eaten raw, either finely sliced in salads, or as a chunk for a snack. Traditionally they are boiled and mashed like potatoes, often with butter and cream added. They lend themselves well to flavourings such as nutmeg, parsley, coriander and black pepper. Swedes are delicious stir-fried, roasted, puréed, steamed, baked, glazed or pickled. Their remarkable ability to absorb flavours makes them ideal additions to soups, stews or casseroles.

AVAILABLE TO PURCHASE
Swedes are available all year round, but they are harder to get in December and January.

Suitable to plant: nationwide although the best swedes are produced in areas that experience cold winters.

When to plant: autumn, spring and summer.

Approx time till harvest: 8–10 weeks. Harvest when young.

Depth to plant: sow seed where you want plants to grow.

Spacing between rows: 30cm.

Spacing between plants: thin seedlings to 7–10cm apart.

Water requirements: water regularly.

Swede with lemon

Swede is wonderfully enhanced by lemon and this succulent lemon glaze is a great way to discover what a fantastic vegetable swede is!

400g swede, peeled and cut into bite sized chunks

1 Tbsp brown sugar

1 Tbsp butter

1 tsp grated lemon rind

2 Tbsp lemon juice

freshly ground black pepper

2 spring onions, thinly sliced diagonally

Place the vegetables, brown sugar, butter, rind, juice and pepper in a microwave-proof dish. Mix, cover and cook on high power for 4–6 minutes or until tender. Stir once during cooking. Garnish with the spring onions. Serves 4.

Sweetcorn

Corn or maize is native to America but is now grown throughout the world. In grain form it is the staple diet for American Indians in Mexico, Peru and Southern North America.

Māori were given maize by American sailors which they grew and ate both fresh and fermented. The fermented corn was known as kaanga. Its strong smell didn't appeal to Pakeha who ate corn mainly as a grain. Eventually a sweet form was developed, and hence the name sweetcorn. It wasn't until the 1960s that sweetcorn became a really popular fresh vegetable. Several varieties are available including some with white kernels and others with a mix of yellow and white kernels. Varieties differ in sweetness. Recently the supersweet varieties have become popular, with Honey 'n' Pearl being the most widely grown.

WHAT TO LOOK FOR

Choose sweetcorn with fresh green husks and soft yellow to light brown tassels. The kernels should be plump, pale and tightly arranged. Sweetcorn varieties come in varying sweetness and colour – yellow and white and sometimes bi-coloured. There is no consistent relationship between colour and sweetness, but the darker the colour the greater presence of carotenoids.

HOW TO KEEP

Refrigerate in plastic bags. Use as soon as you've bought them if you can.

NUTRITIONAL VALUE

Sweetcorn contains a wide range of nutrients including zinc, iron, selenium, potassium, vitamin C and some B group vitamins – folate, thiamine, riboflavin. Significant amounts of vitamin A are made in the body from provitamin A. Of the phytochemicals found in corn the ones with the most interest are lutein and zeaxanthin due to their related activity in eye health. The strong antioxidant activity is due to these carotenoids; phenolics are also present. Sweetcorn is also a valuable source of fibre, protein and starch. It has more protein than most other vegetables.

HOW TO PREPARE

To cook sweetcorn by boiling, remove the husk and tassels and put in boiling water. By the time the water has returned to boiling the corn will be cooked. Overcooking makes the corn go tough. The kernels can be removed with a sharp knife for use in salads and other dishes. To make your own cream corn, remove the kernels with a grater. Sweetcorn is delicious cooked in the husk on a barbecue or in a microwave. Each cob takes 2–3 minutes on 100% power in the microwave. Remove the husk and tassel when the sweetcorn is cool enough.

WAYS TO EAT THIS VEGETABLE

Corn is often eaten cooked with a smidgen of butter or oil – this is great because carotenoids are fat soluble, which means that they are best absorbed into the body when eaten in a meal where some sort of 'healthy' fat or oil is present.

AVAILABLE TO PURCHASE

You can buy fresh sweetcorn from January until April.

Crazy corn cobs

Cooking the corn inside its husk like this seems to make it taste better!

1 cob of corn per person

Place the entire corn cob in the microwave oven (including husk). Cook on high power allowing 2½–3 minutes per cob. Allow to stand for 5 minutes – this gives sufficient time for the corn to cool down enough to handle it. Peel the husk back to form a handle, trim to 10cm. Lightly spread with butter or margarine if you wish.

TIPS
FOR HOME
GARDENERS

Suitable to plant: nationwide.

When to plant: plant in mid to late spring when the weather is warm and settled.

Approx time till harvest: 8–10 weeks.

Depth to plant: 5cm.

Spacing between rows: 50–60cm apart.

Spacing between plants: 20–30cm apart.

Water requirements: water thoroughly at least twice a week in the late spring and summer.

Taro

The taro has helped provide good nutrition to Pacific Islanders for hundreds of years. It is known by several names, taro, talo, dalo. Varieties of taro vary in colour and size. Taro is a starchy root crop and the leaves are also edible.

Taro is not grown commercially in New Zealand; all supplies are imported from the Pacific Islands. Taro has been included in this manual of New Zealand vegetables purely because of its huge following.

Palusami

Palusami are traditionally served with any meat or fish dish, together with baked taro and cassava, or kumara, or green bananas.

32 medium-size clean taro leaves (4 per parcel)

4 cups corned beef, heated and fat drained off

2 onions, peeled and finely diced

2 courgette, grated

4 cups silver beet, chopped

1 cup coconut milk

aluminium foil

Prepare taro leaves by rinsing well. Shake off excess water. For each leaf, remove the tip, all of the stalk, and 1 cm of the leaf around the stalk. Layer 4 taro leaves overlapping each other to form a leak-proof circular shape on and around the aluminium foil. Place some of the meat as a heap in the middle of the taro leaves. Sprinkle some of the onions, courgette and silver beet over the meat. Gather and hold the edges of the taro leaves layer up

forming a bowl then pour the coconut cream on and around the meat. Quickly fold the taro leaves edges inwards to overlap and enclose the palusami. Fold the aluminium foil edges inwards to overlap and enclose the palusami. Place in an oven dish and bake at 200° for one hour. Serve with taro, celery sticks, tomato and lettuce. Serves 8.

Variations:

One of the following may be added as part of the parcel filling:

shrimps

fresh fish

canned fish

lean mince, with the fat drained off

lean pork pieces, precooked in water and onion (if this option is used, omit the coconut milk)

WHAT TO LOOK FOR
When taro is fresh the skin looks healthy and slightly moist. Avoid taro with dry or soft patches on the skin.

HOW TO KEEP
Store in a cool dark, well-ventilated place.

NUTRITIONAL VALUE
Taro roots are high in starch and consequently are one of the highest vegetable sources of energy. They are a very good source of fibre and contain potassium, a little vitamin C and some zinc, thiamin and folate.

HOW TO PREPARE
Wash taro well. It can be scraped and peeled but leave the skin on if possible. Cut into similar sized pieces so that they'll cook at the same rate. Taro contains calcium oxalates in the form of needle-shaped crystals. This causes irritation and a burning sensation if the vegetable is handled or eaten raw. Consequently the use of gloves is often suggested when preparing this vegetable, and long cooking is necessary to destroy these compounds.

WAYS TO EAT THIS VEGETABLE
The traditional ways to cook taro are roasting on stones or baking in a ground oven. More modern ways are boiling and steaming, or baking in an oven. Taro retains its food value if cooked whole and in its skin. It must be cooked thoroughly to prevent your mouth and throat itching. This is caused by a substance called calcium oxalate which is in raw taro. The leaves can make your mouth itch too if not cooked properly. They should be boiled, then drained and then reboiled in fresh water or coconut cream (diluted with milk if you wish). Taro can be used instead of potato or kumara in recipes.

AVAILABLE TO PURCHASE
Taro is imported from the Pacific Islands and is available all year round.

Tomatoes

Tomatoes are native to South America and were originally grown for their decorative purposes. The tomato is actually a fruit but is considered a vegetable because of its uses. Tomatoes belong to the nightshade family along with potatoes, egg plant, tobacco and peppers. They are all distantly related to deadly nightshade and for this reason were for a long time thought to be poisonous. This fear was gradually overcome and by the 19th century they were very popular. They were affectionately known as pommes d'amour by the French, or apples of love. Today consumption of fresh and processed tomatoes is second to potatoes.

All New Zealand tomatoes are ripened on the vine which makes them tastier than some imported varieties which are ripened using ethylene gas. Sometimes New Zealand growers use a product to speed up ripening at the end of the crop, but this is done while the fruit is still on the vine so no flavour is lost.

Recent research has indicated that lycopene, a carotenoid with potent antioxidant effects which is found in raw tomatoes, may be responsible for protection against cancers. This is possibly the reason why people living in the Mediterranean who eat lots of tomatoes have a lower rate of some cancers.

Varieties:
The range of specialty and pre-packed tomatoes has increased dramatically recently. Most tomato varieties are of Dutch origin and are selected for flavour, quality, colour and size. There are a lot of varieties of standard tomatoes, however these tend not to be identified at purchase. Whilst there are exceptions, loose tomatoes tend to be sold in the North Island with the calyx (green stem) removed and in the South Island with the calyx on!

Vine tomatoes
Tomatoes on the vine, or on the truss, are enjoying a huge surge in popularity. Small, medium and large tomatoes are sold on the truss. There are many different vine varieties. As a general rule, vine varieties have a very intense flavour.

Cherry or cocktail tomatoes
These have a sweet intense flavour and are particularly popular with children. Several different varieties are on the market. Coloured red or yellow, the shapes can vary from round, oval to pear-shaped. Small plum tomatoes are particularly sweet and higher in acid.

Low acid tomatoes

Often called acid-free, these have firmer flesh and fewer pips and less juice. They are generally oval, and often misshapen and unevenly coloured with a more pinky colour than ripe red. These come in differing shapes and sizes. Levels of acid vary with variety and no tomato is entirely acid-free.

Plum tomatoes

These tomatoes are a fleshy fruit, oval or plum shaped and usually medium sized. Many plum varieties are low in acid, although not all. Large plum varieties are often referred to as Roma.

Outdoor tomatoes

These make up a very small percentage (around 1%) of the total tomato crop and tend to be less firm than greenhouse grown tomatoes and have a lumpier and flatter shape.

TIPS
FOR HOME
GARDENERS

Suitable to plant: nationwide.

When to plant: spring and summer.

Approx time till harvest: 6–8 weeks.

Depth to plant: 10cm.

Spacing between rows: 50cm depending on the variety.

Spacing between plants: 30–50cm.

Water requirements: water sparingly until the first set of fruit, then weekly after that.

WHAT TO LOOK FOR
Choose smooth, firm and plump tomatoes with an even colour and no blemishes.

HOW TO KEEP
Tomatoes should be stored at room temperature out of direct sunlight. Tomatoes will ripen in these conditions. You can speed up ripening by putting them in a paper bag.
Do not refrigerate unless they are over-ripe. Refrigerated tomatoes do not have the full flavour of tomatoes stored at room temperature.

NUTRITIONAL VALUE
Tomatoes are a very good source of vitamin C, vitamins A and B group, and a good source of fibre. They also provide some vitamin E, folic acid, potassium and other trace elements. Protein and dietary fibre are also present. Tomatoes contain many different antioxidants. One of the most well known is lycopene, which is one of the carotenoids present in tomatoes. The health benefits of lycopene are well documented as it is a particularly powerful antioxidant.

HOW TO PREPARE
Sometimes recipes might suggest you remove the skin and even the seeds of the tomato. Unless this is for a very fine sauce, this generally isn't necessary as most New Zealanders enjoy the taste and texture of the complete tomato.

WAYS TO EAT THIS VEGETABLE
Tomatoes are very versatile and easily prepared. Eat them raw in salads and sandwiches or cooked on pizzas, in a pasta sauce, in casseroles, grilled or baked. Tomatoes are great in soups, omelettes and roulade. Tomatoes preserve well and are easily frozen and bottled. They are delicious when made into homemade sauces, chutneys and are particularly nice when sundried. Tomatoes are complemented by many herbs, especially basil.

AVAILABLE TO PURCHASE
Available all year round.

Slow oven roasted tomatoes

If you are a fan of sun-dried tomatoes then you will adore these – they have all the taste of sun-dried but none of the tough texture! Fantastic!

tomatoes

sea salt

freshly ground black pepper

olive oil

Prepare as many tomatoes as you wish. They may be stored packed in olive oil for 5–7 days in the refrigerator – but I'd be surprised if you have any left over!

Cut the tomatoes in half and place in a single layer in a roasting pan. Sprinkle with sea salt, freshly ground black pepper and drizzle with a little olive oil. Bake at 150°C for 1½ hours (or 1 hour in a fan-forced oven). The tomatoes should retain their shape, but be shrivelled, highly coloured and fragrant. Allow to cool and serve at room temperature.

Turnips

Turnips have been a popular vegetable since Roman times. This white root is a prized vegetable in many cuisines and is used a lot in French and Japanese cooking. Varieties vary in size and shape with roots being generally round or a flattened globe shape. Turnips have a delicate flavour and are best eaten when young and tender. Older turnips have a stronger flavour.

WHAT TO LOOK FOR
Choose small to medium firm roots with smooth skins. Those sized from about 5cm diameter up to the size of a tennis ball will give a delicate peppery taste.

HOW TO KEEP
Refrigerate in plastic bags.

NUTRITIONAL VALUE
Turnips are a good source of calcium and also contain some vitamin C and fibre. Turnips are a member of the brassica family and contain many phytochemicals, particularly the phytosterols and glucosinolates.

HOW TO PREPARE
Turnips don't need to be peeled if they are young and fresh. Late autumn and winter supplies tend to be larger and are stronger in flavour. Their skins are sometimes a bit stringy and peeling is recommended. Turnips are suited to steaming, microwaving, baking and roasting, as well as the more commonly used boiling. They also taste great in a stir-fry when sliced finely and served when still slightly crisp.

WAYS TO EAT THIS VEGETABLE
Turnips, like swede, can be eaten raw but tend to be eaten cooked as a side vegetable or used in savoury dishes such as soups and casseroles. Turnips are particularly suited to being served in a light honey or sugar glaze.

AVAILABLE TO PURCHASE
You can buy turnips from February until August but their main growing season is from March until July.

Suitable to plant: nationwide, however the best turnips are produced where the winters are cold.

When to plant: spring, summer and autumn.

Approx time till harvest: 8 –10 weeks.

Depth to plant: sow seed where you want plants to grow.

Spacing between rows: 30cm.

Spacing between plants: 10–12cm.

Water requirements: water frequently in hot weather. Turnips need constant supplies of moisture if they are to be sweet and crunchy.

Crunchy munchy turnips

Baby turnips are pretty to look at and delicious to eat. This is a very easy way to prepare them.

8–12 baby turnips, washed and trimmed

1 cup water

½ cup finely diced red or yellow pepper

1 Tbsp olive or avocado oil

1 tsp sugar

¼ tsp cumin seeds (optional)

freshly ground black pepper

Place the turnips in a saucepan with the water, bring to the boil, cover, and simmer for 7 minutes. Drain off the water and add the diced peppers, oil, sugar and cumin. Shake the pan to coat the turnips, cover and allow to sit for 2–3 minutes before serving. Season to taste with the freshly ground black pepper. Serves 4.

Watercress

For many years watercress has grown in our streams and ditches. It is only in recent years that it has been grown commercially. The dark green leaves have a peppery flavour and are widely used in salads and sandwiches. They also make an attractive garnish.

WHAT TO LOOK FOR

Choose fresh looking bunches with healthy stems. The leaves should be green, showing no signs of yellowing or wilting.

HOW TO KEEP

Refrigerate in plastic bags. Alternatively, if the roots are still attached, place in a jar of water and do not refrigerate. Use promptly.

NUTRITIONAL VALUE

Watercress is a good source of calcium, fibre and vitamins A and C. It is rich in core nutrients and phytochemicals – particularly glucosinolates which are converted to different isothiocyanates.

HOW TO PREPARE

Discard only the very coarse stalks; these may be added to stocks and soups for extra flavour. Wash well and use the medium to thin stalks and the leaves.

WAYS TO EAT THIS VEGETABLE

Watercress is mostly eaten raw in salads, sandwiches or used as an edible garnish. It is just as tasty when cooked in soups and sauces. It can be used like spinach in omelettes, quiches and pancake fillings.

AVAILABLE TO PURCHASE

Watercress is available all year round with most plentiful supplies from May until December.

TIPS FOR HOME GARDENERS

Suitable to plant: nationwide in sheltered parts of the garden.

When to plant: spring, summer and autumn.

Approx time till harvest: 6–8 weeks.

Depth to plant: 5–10cm.

Spacing between rows: N/A

Spacing between plants: 50cm.

Water requirements: fill a pot that has plenty of drainage holes with a mixture of 50/50 compost and sphagnum moss. Place in a bucket or bowl of water. Watercress grows best when the soil is completely saturated.

Caramelised roast salad

All sorts of vegetables roast well – once you have mastered this recipe experiment with different combinations of onions, peppers, yams, kumara, parsnip, potatoes, beetroot or carrots – even green vegetables, like beans, courgettes or asparagus, taste superb.

2 onions, peeled and cut into wedges

12 mushrooms

3 beetroot, unpeeled and cut into wedges

2 golden kumara, unpeeled and cut into thin (2–3mm) slabs

4 lean venison sausages

¼ cup oil

¼ cup honey or brown sugar

½ cup lemon juice or white vinegar

1 bunch watercress

Place the prepared vegetables and sausages in a baking dish. Blend the oil, honey and lemon juice together. Pour over and mix well. Bake, uncovered in a hot oven for 45–55 minutes or until the kumara is golden and tender. Turn during cooking.

Place the watercress on each serving plate and top with the roasted vegetables. Pour ¼ cup boiling water into the roasting pan, stir to loosen the cooking juices, pour over the salad. Serves 4.

Witloof

Witloof is a Dutch name which translates as white leaf. The name of this vegetable is a bit confusing. In New Zealand we call it either witloof or chicory, the British call it chicory and the French call it endive or Belgium endive. To make it even more confusing there is a type of lettuce which the French call chicory and which is known as endive in Britain and New Zealand.

Witloof have a slightly bitter and nutty flavour. The leaves have been eaten for thousands of years and the roots in some strains are used as a coffee substitute.

Radicchio

This is a red-leafed variety related to witloof. It is very popular overseas and is available in limited quantities in New Zealand. Radicchio adds both an interesting colour and taste to winter salads.

WHAT TO LOOK FOR
Look for crisp, firm, compact heads which are creamy white with pale yellow tips.

HOW TO KEEP
Refrigerate in plastic bags. Use as soon as possible.

NUTRITIONAL VALUE
Witloof supplies useful amounts of vitamin A, fibre, potassium, calcium and iron.

HOW TO PREPARE
Witloof is grown in the dark and needs to be stored away from the light otherwise it will go bitter. Trim the stalk end before you use it and remove any damaged outer leaves.

WAYS TO EAT THIS VEGETABLE
Witloof can be eaten raw as a salad vegetable and is ideal to mix with other salad greens. It can also be braised whole or sliced, and served with different sauces. Stuffed, curried or baked with ham, witloof also goes well with cheese and is great in flans and pies. It is good when sliced into stir-fries.

AVAILABLE TO PURCHASE
Witloof can be bought from May until October.

TIPS
FOR HOME
GARDENERS

Suitable to plant: nationwide.

When to plant: spring, summer and autumn.

Approx time till harvest: 4–6 months from planting.

Depth to plant: 5cm.

Spacing between rows: 50–60cm.

Spacing between plants: 50cm.

Water requirements: water well in summer, less in winter when the endive chicons, (witloof) are being prepared.

Witloof and orange salad

The sophisticated slightly bitter, yet nutty, flavour of the witloof is complemented by the sweetness of the the orange. If the oranges are nice and juicy you don't need a dressing.

2 witloof

2 oranges, peeled and sliced

¼ cup pistachio nuts

70g blue cheese, finely sliced

2 spring onions, finely sliced

Separate the leaves of the witloof and arrange on a plate. Top with the orange slices, pistachio nuts, blue cheese and spring onions. Serves 4.

Yams

The yams that are grown in New Zealand originate from the South American Andes where they are an important vegetable crop known as oca. The sweet tubers are quite small, often about the size of your thumb. They are pink-orange in colour and have a slightly shiny and ribbed surface. Other varieties which are sweeter, slightly smaller and coloured yellow, apricot and golden are available. New Zealand yams are very different from the tropical yams grown in other cultures. In America, and hence American recipe books, the vegetables known as 'yams' are in fact sweet potatoes like our Beauregard kumara.

Earth gems

Earth gems are not related to yams, however their use is very similar. Earth gems are known as ulluco in their native South America and have only been commercially available in New Zealand since 2003. The brightly coloured tubers range from yellow to magenta, pink, and even candy striped. They are very small in size, about 2–3cm in diameter. Their waxy skins are so shiny and colourful that they have been likened to botanical jewels. Their skin is thin and soft and needs no peeling before eating. The white to lemon-yellow flesh has a smooth, silky texture with a nutty taste, similar to beetroot. Earth gems have a crisp texture, which remains even when cooked. Earth gems can be boiled, steamed, microwaved or baked and served as a side vegetable. They hold their colour after cooking and look very attractive on the plate. With high levels of vitamin C they are an excellent choice for winter dining. Availability is from June until October.

WHAT TO LOOK FOR
Firm yams with a bright colour and no blemishes are the best.

HOW TO KEEP
Refrigerate in plastic bags.

NUTRITIONAL VALUE
Yams contain useful amounts of vitamin A, vitamin B6, fibre and potassium. They also contribute small amounts of riboflavin, thiamine and potassium. The almost fluorescent colours of yams indicate the presence of carotenoids (yellow colours) and anthocyanins (red skins and specks in the flesh). Yams also contain oxalates.

HOW TO PREPARE
Don't peel yams. Scrub them if necessary and remove any blemishes. All yams are eaten cooked and it is in the cooked form that the carotenoids are more available. Yams are always eaten with the skin on which is great because anthocyanins and fibre are present in the skin. Boiling or steaming minimise the oxalate levels.

WAYS TO EAT THIS VEGETABLE
As a side vegetable yams are great baked or microwaved with a little lemon juice, butter and a sprinkling of brown sugar. Yams are good roasted or added to potato wedges. They are also able to be steamed or boiled and can be served whole or mashed. A yam cooked for 40–50 seconds in the microwave makes a good snack for small children. Sliced yams are great in stir-fries, especially if still slightly crisp. Lightly cooked and sliced with a lemon or lime vinaigrette dressing, yams make a great salad base. The natural sweetness of the yams makes them really good to use with ginger, orange or sweet and sour sauces.

AVAILABLE TO PURCHASE
You can buy yams from June until October, with limited quantities available in late autumn.

Suitable to plant: nationwide however plants resent both cold frosty and hot weather.

When to plant: spring when the tubers begin to sprout.

Approx time till harvest: 4–6 months.

Depth to plant: 10–15cm deep in a free-draining soil.

Spacing between rows: 50cm.

Spacing between plants: 50cm.

Water requirements: water well during dry periods.

Yams with lime

Very simple and very delicious – the tang of the lime goes so well with the natural sweetness of the yams. If you haven't got limes use lemons.

400g yams, halved lengthwise
1 Tbsp brown sugar
1 Tbsp olive oil
1 tsp grated lime rind
2 Tbsp lime juice
freshly ground black pepper
1 Tbsp finely chopped fresh mint or parsley

Place the vegetables, brown sugar, oil, rind, juice and pepper in a microwave-proof dish. Mix, cover and cook on high power for 4–6 minutes or until tender. Stir once during cooking. Mix the herbs through the vegetables. Serves 4.

Recipes

For more delicious ways to use vegetables visit **www.vegetables.co.nz**